Voyages in Vans

A Traveler's Guide to RV Life in National Parks

Peter Wilson

Table of Contents

INTRODUCTION

It is an interesting and thorough guidebook that caters to the adventurous spirit of RV travelers eager to discover national parks' natural beauty. "Voyages in Vans: A Traveler's Guide to RV Life in National Parks" is a guidebook that is an excellent choice for those individuals. This book is a wonderful resource of knowledge, insights, and recommendations for people who are new to exploring this one-of-a-kind mode of travel as well as those who have been RVing for years.

The book is, at its core, a celebration of the freedom and joy that comes with life on the road, with a particular emphasis on the great national parks that are located across a variety of locations. From choosing the appropriate vehicle and equipment to gaining a grasp of the complexities involved in navigating diverse terrains, the author delves into the practical aspects of traveling in a recreational vehicle (RV). There is a plethora of information available regarding how to make the most efficient use of space in a van, how to keep the vehicle in pristine shape, and how to guarantee a trip that is both safe and fun.

The book's investigation of national parks in great depth is the most important part of the title. The parks are brought to life through evocative descriptions that highlight the distinctive landscapes, fauna, and recreational activities that each park offers. The guide provides useful information such as the best times to visit, camping places, and attractions that are a must-see, in addition to providing ideas that are less well-known but may be used to make the experience more enjoyable.

A personal touch is added by the use of photography and personal experiences from the author as well as other RV enthusiasts. This gives the reader the impression that they are a part of a bigger community of travelers. In addition, the book discusses the difficulties that come with living in an RV, providing answers to the most prevalent issues as well as guidance on how to live in a sustainable manner while traveling.

The book "Voyages in Vans" is more than simply a travel guide; it is also a source of motivation for people who have a desire to live a life that is not just ordinary, one that is full of the wonders of nature and the excitement of discovery. An invitation to go on a journey in which the journey itself is the destination is being extended before you. This book is an indispensable companion for anybody who has ever fantasized about living a life filled with excitement and adventure on the open road.

CHAPTER I

Introduction to RV Life

The allure of RV travel

Over the past few years, there has been a spike in the popularity of traveling in recreational vehicles (RVs), which has captured the imagination of those who are equally interested in adventuring and wandering. The attractiveness of traveling in a recreational vehicle (RV) rests in the fact that it provides a one-of-a-kind combination of independence, flexibility, and comfort. It provides a transforming experience that enables users to explore the world on their own terms. This section will dig into the different aspects that make RV travel so alluring, from the opportunity to enjoy the great outdoors to the sense of community that it generates, eventually showcasing its enduring charm in today's fast-paced world. RV travel is something that has been gaining popularity in recent years.

The flexibility that comes with traveling in a recreational vehicle is one of the most appealing aspects of this kind of transportation. Those who are passionate about recreational vehicles have the freedom to travel at their own speed, selecting their locations and routes as they go along by themselves. The necessity to adhere to strict schedules or rush through crowded airports is not something that must be done. Travelers, on the other hand, have the opportunity to relish the journey itself, pausing anywhere and whenever they choose to soak in stunning scenery, hidden gems, and unexpected adventures. This sense of liberty is appealing to individuals who yearn for a break from the restraints of daily life, since it enables them to break free from the confines of a traditional vacation.

Moreover, traveling in a recreational vehicle provides an unrivaled opportunity to reestablish a connection with the natural world. It gives tourists the opportunity to completely submerge themselves in the splendor of unspoiled landscapes, ranging from the peaceful quiet of national parks to the rough charm of mountain ranges and seaside vistas. It is a deep and refreshing experience to have the opportunity to escape into the woods in this day that is controlled by screens and concrete jungles. It is possible for tourists to enjoy the great outdoors without losing the conveniences of contemporary life by renting a recreational vehicle (RV), which offers a home on wheels that is both comfortable and self-sufficient. This combination of ease of use and natural beauty is a potent magnet for people who are looking to develop a more profound connection with the natural world.

The attractiveness of traveling in a recreational vehicle (RV) is not confined to its connection to the natural world; it also helps travelers feel more connected to one another. Recreational vehicle (RV) enthusiasts frequently find themselves in the company of other people who share their enthusiasm for traveling and discovering new places. There is a strong sense of camaraderie that prevails in campgrounds, RV parks, and common spaces, which become hubs for social interaction characterized by the exchange of stories, the formation of friendships, and the formation of friendships. The recreational vehicle (RV) community is inclusive for people of all ages and walks of life, and they are tied together by their shared passion for traveling. Every voyage is an opportunity to build new relationships, and it is a place where people who are not familiar with one other can become friends.

Additionally, traveling in a recreational vehicle (RV) is a way of exploration that promotes personal development and self-discovery. In the process of venturing beyond their comfort zones and embarking on activities that are unexpected to them, travelers are presented with new challenges and experiences that improve their lived experiences. Problem-solving abilities, adaptability, and a sense of self-reliance are all developed via the process of planning routes, setting up camp, and navigating the road. It encourages people to be more open to serendipity, to value the trip more than the destination, and to take pleasure in the moment that they are currently experiencing.

A further facet of the attractiveness of traveling in a recreational vehicle is the economic and practical benefits it offers. Traveling in a recreational vehicle (RV) is a cost-effective method of transportation because it eliminates the need to stay in expensive motels and eat out every night. People who are traveling have the ability to prepare their own meals and select campgrounds that are favorable to their wallets, which enables them to stretch their vacation budget even further. Additionally, RV travel is an appealing choice for families, retirees, and anybody else who is looking for a home away from home because of the comfort and convenience of having all requirements within arm's reach.

Despite the fact that traveling in an RV fosters a sense of independence and freedom, it also makes it possible to be flexible with one's travel plans. RV travelers have the ability to change their plans on a whim, in contrast to traditional vacationers who are constrained by obligations such as flight timetables and hotel reservations. They are able to extend their stay if they find a particular location that captivates their heart; if an unforeseen chance presents itself, they are able to grasp it without having to worry about finding a place to stay. The ability to be flexible is a luxury that is hard to come by in today's environment, where time is frequently a valuable commodity.

In conclusion, the ability of recreational vehicles (RVs) to provide a one-of-a-kind combination of independence, flexibility, comfort, and connection is what makes RV travel so appealing. Through it, travelers are able to break free from the confines of their everyday lives, reestablish meaningful connections with the natural world, forge enduring friendships, and go on journeys of self-improvement. Exploration and adventure are experiencing a rebirth thanks to the development of RV travel, which provides a lifestyle that is not only rewarding but also affordable. The charm of RV travel continues to shine brightly in a world that is yearning for new vistas. This is because more people are looking for a break from the usual and the opportunity to craft their own travel stories.

Benefits of RV life in national parks

National parks are treasured natural wonders that offer a glimpse into our planet's pristine beauty and biodiversity. Each year, millions of visitors flock to these protected areas to experience the majesty of untouched landscapes, the thrill of wildlife encounters, and the tranquility of nature. RV life is an enticing opportunity for those who wish to immerse themselves in the national park experience fully. The benefits of RV life in national parks are numerous and profound, ranging from unparalleled access to remote locations and the ability to enjoy extended stays to the flexibility of exploring at one's own pace. This section will delve into these advantages, shedding light on why RV life is the ideal way to savor the natural splendor of our nation's parks.

One of the most remarkable benefits of RV life in national parks is its unmatched access to remote and less-visited areas. Many national parks are vast, with extensive trail systems and hidden gems tucked away from the crowds. RVs allow travelers to explore these off-the-beaten-path locations, where solitude and serenity reign. Unlike traditional campers who must return to crowded campgrounds at the end of the day, RV dwellers can choose to camp in more remote areas, closer to the heart of the wilderness. This proximity allows them to witness the dawn chorus of birds, the hushed whispers of rustling leaves, and the awe-inspiring starry night skies that city-dwellers can only dream of. RV life unlocks the door to a deeper connection with the natural world.

Furthermore, RV life in national parks offers the luxury of extended stays. The standard two-week vacation hardly does justice to these protected areas' vast and diverse landscapes. RV travelers can stay for weeks or even months, allowing them to absorb the park's offerings at their own pace fully. This extended presence fosters a profound connection with the environment, as RV dwellers become intimately acquainted with the park's rhythms, from the changing seasons to the ebb and flow of wildlife activity. It is not uncommon for RV enthusiasts to become temporary residents of a national park, immersing themselves in the park's wonders and truly becoming a part of the natural tapestry.

Flexibility is another hallmark of RV life in national parks. Unlike rigid travel itineraries that dictate specific dates and times, RV travelers can adapt their plans as the spirit moves them. They can choose to linger in a particularly captivating spot, undertake spontaneous hikes, or explore lesser-known trails without the constraints of hotel check-out times or flight schedules. This adaptability encourages a deeper exploration of the park's nooks and crannies, fostering a sense of discovery and adventure that is not bound by the limitations of traditional travel.

Additionally, RV life in national parks provides a level of comfort and convenience that enhances the overall experience. RVs offer modern amenities such as fully equipped kitchens, bathrooms, and comfortable sleeping quarters, ensuring that travelers have a comfortable and self-sustaining home on wheels. After a day of hiking and exploring, RV dwellers can return to their cozy abode, relax in their own space, and enjoy a hot meal without the need to dine out or endure the inconveniences of traditional camping. This comfort allows travelers to focus more on the park's natural wonders and less on the logistics of their stay.

The sense of community that RV life fosters is another noteworthy benefit. National park campgrounds often become hubs of social interaction, where travelers from diverse backgrounds come together to share stories, experiences, and a love for the outdoors. Bonds are formed around campfires, and friendships are forged over shared adventures. This sense of camaraderie adds a layer of richness to the national park experience, as travelers exchange tips, recommendations, and a mutual appreciation for the natural world.

Furthermore, RV life aligns with the principles of sustainable and responsible travel. RVs are equipped with modern, eco-friendly technologies, such as solar panels and energy-efficient appliances, reducing their environmental impact. RV travelers also tend to be more conscious of their ecological footprint, practicing Leave No Trace principles and respecting the delicate ecosystems of national parks. This commitment to environmental stewardship ensures that these natural wonders are preserved for future generations to enjoy.

In conclusion, RV life in national parks offers a unique and enriching way to experience the splendor of our nation's protected areas. The benefits are manifold, from unparalleled access to remote locations and extended stays that deepen the connection with nature to the flexibility, comfort, and sense of community that RV travel provides. As the allure of national parks continues to draw nature enthusiasts and adventure seekers, RV life remains an ideal way to unlock the full potential of these natural treasures. It is a lifestyle that embodies the spirit of exploration, fostering a profound appreciation for the beauty and wonder of the natural world.

Setting the stage for your journey

Embarking on an RV journey is an exciting and transformative experience that opens up a world of adventure and discovery. Whether you're a seasoned traveler or a novice looking to hit the open road, setting the stage for your RV journey is crucial to ensure a smooth and enjoyable adventure. This section will guide you through the essential steps to prepare for your RV journey, from choosing the right RV and planning your route to packing efficiently and understanding the practical aspects of RV life.

First and foremost, selecting the right RV is a pivotal decision that sets the foundation for your journey. RVs come in various types, each catering to different preferences and needs. Motorhomes, for instance, offer the convenience of an all-in-one vehicle, with living quarters and driving space integrated. On the other hand, travel trailers and fifth wheels can be towed by a separate vehicle, providing more flexibility in terms of transportation once you've set up camp. The choice between a Class A, Class B, or Class C motorhome, or a particular type of travel trailer, depends on factors like your budget, the number of travelers, and the level of comfort and amenities you desire. Conduct thorough research and consider renting an RV for a trial run to determine the best fit for your journey.

Once you've selected your RV, planning your route is the next crucial step. Unlike traditional vacations where flights and hotels dictate your itinerary, RV travel offers the freedom to chart your course. Begin by choosing your destination or destinations. National parks, scenic routes, and historic landmarks are popular choices for RV enthusiasts. Research the routes to your chosen locations, considering the distance, road conditions, and potential stopovers. Online tools and apps can help you plan your journey efficiently, highlighting points of interest, campgrounds, and RV-friendly services along the way. Remember that flexibility is one of the advantages of RV travel, so be prepared to adjust your route to accommodate unexpected discoveries and detours.

Efficient packing is a skill that can significantly enhance your RV journey. While RVs offer more space and storage than traditional vehicles, it's essential to pack wisely to avoid clutter and make the most of your living space. Create a checklist of essentials, including clothing, toiletries, cooking utensils, and outdoor gear. Prioritize items that serve multiple purposes and choose compact and collapsible versions whenever possible. Overpacking can lead to unnecessary weight, affecting fuel efficiency, and making your RV feel cramped. Remember your specific RV model's storage compartments and limitations and aim for a balance between comfort and practicality. Understanding the practical aspects of RV life is crucial for a smooth journey. Familiarize yourself with the RV's systems, including the water, electrical, and sewage systems. Learning how to set up and break down your campsite, including leveling your RV, connecting utilities, and securing it properly, is essential for a stress-free experience. Be aware of campground rules and etiquette, such as quiet hours and waste disposal procedures. Additionally, develop a basic understanding of RV maintenance, from checking tire pressure to regular cleaning and upkeep. Proper maintenance ensures that your RV remains in good condition throughout your journey.

Safety should be a top priority when setting the stage for your RV journey. Inspect your RV thoroughly before departure, checking for any mechanical issues or signs of wear and tear. Ensure that safety equipment such as smoke detectors, fire extinguishers, and carbon monoxide detectors are in working order. Familiarize yourself with the RV's driving characteristics, especially if you're new to handling a larger vehicle. Practice safe driving habits, such as maintaining a safe following distance and being aware of blind spots. Consider taking a defensive driving course if you're not confident in your driving skills. Furthermore, have a first-aid kit on hand and know how to use it and the locations of nearby medical facilities along your route.

Financial planning is another essential aspect of setting the stage for your RV journey. Create a budget that includes expenses such as fuel, campground fees, food, and any activities or attractions you plan to visit. It's essential to have a financial cushion for unexpected costs or emergencies. Keep track of your expenses throughout the journey to ensure you stay within your budget. Additionally, consider ways to save on expenses, such as cooking your meals in the RV instead of dining out frequently and seeking discounts or memberships that can reduce campground fees.

A crucial component of RV travel is embracing the minimalist and sustainable mindset it encourages. RV life encourages travelers to reduce their carbon footprint by conserving resources such as water and electricity. Learning to be mindful of consumption and waste can benefit the environment and enhance your overall RV experience. Invest in reusable products and practice Leave No Trace principles by cleaning up after yourself and respecting the natural areas you visit.

Lastly, setting the stage for your RV journey should involve creating a flexible itinerary that allows you to immerse yourself in the journey rather than simply focusing on the destination. RV travel offers the unique opportunity to explore at your own pace, with the freedom to pause and appreciate the beauty and serenity of unexpected places. Be open to spontaneity and new experiences, and embrace RV life's sense of adventure.

In conclusion, setting the stage for your RV journey is a multifaceted process that requires careful planning, preparation, and a willingness to embrace the unknown. Choosing the right RV, planning your route, packing efficiently, understanding the practical aspects of RV life, prioritizing safety, financial planning, and adopting a minimalist and sustainable mindset are all essential elements of a successful RV adventure. With the proper groundwork, your RV journey can be a transformative experience filled with exploration, self-discovery, and unforgettable memories that will last a lifetime.

CHAPTER II

Choosing the Right RV

Different types of RVs (Motorhomes, Trailers, Campervans)

Recreational vehicles (RVs) have long been a symbol of adventure and freedom on the open road. They offer a unique way to travel and explore the world, providing both transportation and accommodation all in one. RV enthusiasts have a diverse range of options to choose from when it comes to selecting the right type of RV for their needs. The main categories of RVs are motorhomes, trailers, and campervans, each with its own set of features, advantages, and limitations. In this section, we will delve into the different types of RVs, exploring their distinct characteristics and discussing the factors to consider when choosing the perfect RV for your journey.

Motorhomes, often called "RVs" in a general sense, are fully self-contained vehicles that combine driving and living spaces. They come in three primary classes: Class A, Class B, and Class C motorhomes. Class A motorhomes are the largest and most luxurious of the bunch, resembling tour buses with their spacious interiors and all the amenities of a home. They are typically built on heavy-duty chassis and can range from 30 to 45 feet long, making them the go-to choice for those seeking a lavish RV lifestyle. Class A motorhomes often feature slide-out sections, which expand the living space when parked, and they are equipped with amenities such as full kitchens, bathrooms, entertainment systems, and even washer-dryer units.

Class B motorhomes, also known as camper vans, are the smallest in the motorhome family. They are built on van chassis and are compact, easy to maneuver, and versatile. Despite their smaller size, Class B motorhomes offer many of the amenities found in larger RVs, including sleeping quarters, a kitchenette, and a bathroom. Their compact design makes them perfect for solo travelers, couples, or small families looking for a nimble and fuel- efficient RV experience. Class B motorhomes are also favored for their ability to access remote and off-grid locations that may be challenging for larger RVs.

Class C motorhomes balance Class A and Class B in terms of size and amenities. They are built on a van or truck chassis with a cab-over bunk area extending over the driver's compartment. This feature provides additional sleeping space and storage, making Class C motorhomes a popular choice for families. They typically offer a comfortable living area, a well-equipped kitchen, a bathroom, and various entertainment options. Class C motorhomes are more affordable than Class A models while still providing a comfortable and spacious RV experience.

Trailers, however, are towable RVs that require a separate vehicle, typically a truck or SUV, to pull them. They come in various shapes and sizes, with the most common types being travel trailers, fifth-wheel trailers, and pop-up campers. Travel trailers are the most popular and versatile of the trailer options. They range from compact teardrop trailers to spacious models with multiple slide-outs. Travel trailers can accommodate a wide range of floorplans, allowing for customization to fit specific needs. They offer all the amenities of a home, including bedrooms, kitchens, bathrooms, and entertainment areas, making them an excellent choice for families and long-term travelers.

Fifth-wheel trailers are a type of travel trailer that requires a specialized hitch in a pickup truck's bed. This hitch design allows for increased stability and maneuverability while towing. Fifth-wheel trailers often feature luxurious interiors, spacious living areas, and multiple slide-outs, providing a comfortable and homely experience. Their design also allows for split-level floorplans, with a raised front section that can serve as a dedicated bedroom or entertainment space. This type of RV is well-suited for extended vacations and full-time RV living.

Pop-up campers, also known as tent trailers or fold-down campers, are the most compact and lightweight of the trailer options. They are designed to be compact during travel and expandable when parked. Pop-up campers typically include sleeping areas, a small kitchenette, and sometimes a portable toilet. While they offer fewer amenities than other RV types, they are highly portable and cost-effective, making them popular for weekend getaways and camping adventures.

Campervans, often called "Class B motorhomes," are a unique category of RVs that are smaller and more compact than traditional motorhomes. They are built on van chassis and are known for their versatility and ease of maneuverability. Campervans are a popular choice for travelers who want the freedom of the open road without the bulk of a larger RV. They often include basic amenities such as a sleeping area, a kitchenette, and a small bathroom, providing a comfortable and convenient travel experience. Campervans are perfect for solo travelers or couples seeking a nimble and minimalist RV lifestyle.

Several factors should be considered when choosing the right type of RV for your journey. First and foremost is your travel style and preferences. Are you looking for a luxurious and spacious RV experience or prefer a more compact and nimble approach? The number of travelers in your group and the length of your trips will also influence your decision. Families with children may opt for larger RVs with more sleeping space and amenities, while solo travelers or couples may prefer the simplicity of a campervan or a small travel trailer.

Budget is another critical factor. RVs come in a wide price range, from affordable pop-up campers to high-end Class A motorhomes. Setting a budget that aligns with your financial capabilities and long-term travel plans is essential. Additionally, consider the type of terrain and destinations you plan to explore. Some RVs are better suited for off-road adventures, while others excel on highways and well-maintained roads.

Maintenance and storage are practical considerations as well. Larger RVs may require more upkeep and storage space when not in use. Smaller RVs and campervans are easier to maintain and can often be parked in standard driveways or storage facilities.

In conclusion, the world of RVs offers diverse options to cater to every traveler's unique needs and preferences. Motorhomes, trailers, and campervans each come with their own set of advantages and limitations, making it essential to carefully consider your travel style, budget, and destination preferences before making a choice. The ultimate goal is to select an RV that enhances your travel experience, whether it's the freedom of the open road in a Class A motorhome, the versatility of a campervan, or the simplicity of a pop-up camper. Regardless of your choice, embarking on an RV journey promises adventure, exploration, and the opportunity to create lasting memories on the road.

Renting vs. Buying

The allure of RV travel has captured the hearts of many adventurers seeking freedom and flexibility on the open road. One of the crucial decisions that aspiring RV enthusiasts must make is whether to rent or buy an RV. Both options have their advantages and drawbacks, and the choice often hinges on individual preferences, financial considerations, and travel goals. This section will explore the merits and downsides of renting and buying an RV, helping potential RV travelers make an informed decision that aligns with their lifestyle and aspirations.

Renting an RV offers several appealing benefits for those looking to dip their toes into the world of recreational vehicle travel. One of the primary advantages is the lower upfront cost. Renting an RV eliminates the substantial financial commitment required to purchase an RV, which can range from thousands to hundreds of thousands of dollars, depending on the type and size of the vehicle. This financial flexibility allows travelers to experience the joys of RV travel without a substantial initial investment.

Furthermore, renting an RV offers the opportunity to test various types of RVs before committing to a purchase. This is particularly valuable for newcomers to RV travel who are unsure about which RV type and size best suits their needs and preferences. By renting different models, travelers can gain firsthand experience and insight into the features, layouts, and amenities that work best for them. It's a valuable learning experience that can help prevent costly mistakes when eventually purchasing an RV.

Maintenance and upkeep are also less burdensome for renters. RV ownership comes with responsibilities such as regular maintenance, insurance, and storage when not in use. On the other hand, renters can simply return the RV to the rental company at the end of their trip, leaving behind the hassles of maintenance and repair. This is especially attractive to those who want to enjoy the RV lifestyle without the long-term commitment and responsibilities associated with ownership.

Another perk of renting is its flexibility in choosing the right RV for each trip. Travelers can select the size and type of RV that best suits the specific journey they have in mind. A larger RV with more amenities may be ideal if a cross-country road trip is on the agenda. Conversely, a smaller RV or campervan may be better suited for shorter getaways or trips to more remote locations. Renters can tailor their choice to match the adventure, allowing for a more customized and comfortable travel experience.

On the downside, renting an RV can be expensive, especially for extended trips. Rental costs can add up quickly, encompassing the daily or weekly rental fee and additional expenses such as insurance, mileage fees, cleaning fees, and fuel costs. For travelers planning frequent or extended RV journeys, these expenses can become a significant part of their budget. In the long run, the cumulative rental costs may approach or even exceed the price of purchasing an RV.

Moreover, rental availability can be challenging, especially during peak travel seasons. RV rental companies often experience high demand during summer months and holiday seasons, leading to limited availability and higher prices. This can result in the need to book rental RVs well in advance, potentially limiting spontaneity and flexibility in travel plans.

Buying an RV, on the other hand, offers a different set of advantages and drawbacks. One of the most significant benefits is the sense of ownership and the potential for long-term cost savings. While the initial purchase price of an RV is substantial, owning an RV allows travelers to amortize the cost over multiple trips and years of use. Over time, the cost per trip can be significantly lower than renting, making ownership an attractive option for those planning frequent and extended RV travel.

Ownership also provides a sense of familiarity and personalization. Owners can customize their RV to suit their preferences, adding personal touches and upgrades that enhance their travel experience. This level of control and comfort can contribute to a more enjoyable and rewarding journey.

Additionally, owning an RV means having the flexibility to hit the road whenever the desire arises, without the need to coordinate with rental companies or adhere to strict rental schedules. Travelers can embark on spontaneous trips, explore off-the-beaten-path destinations, and extend their journeys as they see fit. This freedom to travel on a whim is a significant draw for RV enthusiasts.

However, RV ownership is not without its challenges and responsibilities. The upfront cost of an RV can be a substantial financial burden, and it's essential to consider the purchase price and ongoing expenses such as insurance, maintenance, storage, and campground fees. These costs can add up, making ownership a more significant financial commitment in the long term.

Maintenance and upkeep are among the most critical responsibilities of RV ownership. Regular maintenance is essential to keep the RV in good working condition, and repair costs can be significant, especially for older or more complex RVs. Owners must also find suitable storage for their RV when it's not in use, which can be a challenge for those without ample space on their property.

Depreciation is another factor to consider when buying an RV. Like most vehicles, RVs depreciate in value over time, and the depreciation rate can vary depending on factors such as the RV's age, condition, and market demand. Owners should be prepared for the possibility of a lower resale value when they decide to sell their RV.

In conclusion, renting or buying an RV hinges on individual preferences, financial considerations, and travel goals. Renting offers a lower upfront cost, flexibility in RV selection, and relief from maintenance and storage responsibilities. It's an ideal choice for those looking to test the waters of RV travel or for travelers who prefer the convenience of renting for shorter trips.

On the other hand, buying an RV provides a sense of ownership, long-term cost savings, and the ability to customize and personalize the RV. It offers the freedom to travel on a whim and the potential for a lower cost per trip over time. However, it comes with a significant initial investment, ongoing expenses, and maintenance and storage responsibilities.

Ultimately, the decision between renting and buying an RV should be based on careful consideration of one's financial situation, travel preferences, and the frequency and duration of RV trips. Both options offer the opportunity to experience the joys of RV travel, and the choice should align with the individual's unique circumstances and aspirations. Whether renting or buying, embarking on an RV journey promises adventure, exploration, and the chance to create lasting memories on the road.

Factors to consider when selecting an RV

Selecting the right recreational vehicle (RV) is a pivotal decision for those seeking the freedom and adventure of the open road. Whether embarking on cross-country road trips, exploring national parks, or simply enjoying weekend getaways, the choice of RV can significantly impact the overall travel experience. There is a wide range of RV types, sizes, and features to choose from, each catering to different needs and preferences. To make an informed decision, it's essential to consider various factors that encompass everything from your travel style and budget to the type of destinations you plan to explore.

The first and most crucial factor to consider is your travel style and purpose. Are you planning to take short weekend getaways, extended road trips, or even live in your RV full-time? Your travel style and purpose will dictate the type and size of RV that best suits your needs. For example, solo travelers or couples may find campervans or smaller trailers ideal for weekend escapes, while families or retirees embarking on long journeys might prefer larger motorhomes or fifth-wheel trailers with more living space and amenities.

Another critical consideration is your budget. RVs come in a wide range of price points, from affordable pop-up campers to high-end Class A motorhomes. Establishing a clear budget is essential, considering the purchase price and ongoing costs such as insurance, maintenance, and campground fees. Finding an RV that aligns with your financial capabilities while still meeting your travel requirements is essential.

The size and layout of the RV are significant considerations. Smaller RVs are easier to maneuver and park, making them suitable for those seeking versatility and access to remote locations. Larger RVs offer more living space and amenities, providing a comfortable and homely experience. Consider the number of travelers in your group, your desired sleeping arrangements, and the overall living space when evaluating size and layout options.

RVs have various amenities and features that can significantly enhance your travel experience. Common amenities include kitchens, bathrooms, entertainment systems, slide-out sections, and storage space. Determine which amenities are essential for your journey and which ones you can do without. For example, a well-equipped kitchen may be a priority if you enjoy cooking, while others may prioritize a spacious bathroom or comfortable sleeping arrangements.

RV ownership comes with maintenance and upkeep responsibilities. Regular maintenance is essential to keep the RV in good working condition, and repair costs can vary depending on the RV's age and complexity. Assessing your willingness and ability to perform or finance maintenance tasks is essential. If maintenance is a concern, you may opt to rent an RV or choose a newer model with a warranty.

When not in use, RVs require suitable storage. Consider where you will store your RV when it's not on the road. Some options include keeping it in your driveway, renting storage space, or finding RV-friendly storage facilities. The availability of storage options in your area can influence your choice of RV.

If you plan to tow a trailer, it's crucial to ensure that your tow vehicle has the appropriate towing capacity. Exceeding your vehicle's towing capacity can lead to safety issues and additional wear and tear on your vehicle. Consult your vehicle's manual or a professional to determine its towing limits and choose a trailer that falls within those limits.

Fuel efficiency varies among different types of RVs. Larger motorhomes and fifth-wheel trailers typically have lower fuel efficiency than smaller, more aerodynamic models like campervans or travel trailers. Consider the impact of fuel costs on your budget and environmental concerns when selecting an RV.

If you plan to venture off the beaten path and explore rugged or remote terrain, the off-road capability of your RV becomes crucial. Some RVs are better suited for off-road adventures, with features like four-wheel drive, higher ground clearance, and reinforced suspensions. Others are designed primarily for on-road travel. Assess your intended destinations and the level of off-road capability you need.

RVs, like most vehicles, depreciate in value over time. If you anticipate selling your RV in the future, consider its resale value. Some RV brands and models hold their value better than others. Research potential RVs' depreciation rates and resale values to make an informed decision.

Before making a final decision, read user reviews and seek recommendations from experienced RV travelers. Online forums, RV clubs, and social media groups are valuable resources where you can learn from others' experiences and gain insights into specific RV models and brands.
Take the RV for a test drive or rent a similar model for a short trip whenever possible. This hands-on experience will give you a feel for the RV's handling, comfort, and functionality, helping you determine if it's the right fit for your needs.

Safety should always be a top priority when selecting an RV. Check for essential safety features such as airbags, anti-lock brakes, stability control systems, and tire pressure monitoring. Additionally, ensure that the RV meets safety standards and regulations for recreational vehicles.
Consider the warranty offered by the manufacturer. Warranties can vary in duration and coverage, so it's essential to understand what is included and for how long. A solid warranty can provide peace of mind and financial protection in case of unexpected issues.

In conclusion, choosing the right RV involves a comprehensive assessment of your travel style, budget, preferences, and practical needs. The decision should be guided by careful consideration of these factors, ensuring that your RV enhances your travel experience and aligns with your goals. Whether you opt for a compact campervan, a spacious motorhome, or anything in between, embarking on an RV journey promises adventure, exploration, and the opportunity to create lasting memories on the open road.

CHAPTER III

Planning Your RV Adventure

Researching national parks

Embarking on an RV trip to explore national parks' natural beauty and wonder is a dream for many adventure seekers. With many breathtaking landscapes, diverse ecosystems, and unique wildlife, national parks offer a chance to reconnect with nature, experience the great outdoors, and create lasting memories. However, a successful national park RV trip requires careful planning and thorough research. This section will delve into the essential aspects of researching national parks for an RV adventure, from choosing the suitable parks and understanding park regulations to planning your itinerary and enjoying a safe and memorable journey.

The first step in planning your RV trip to national parks is selecting the right parks to visit. The United States boasts a wide range of national parks, each with its distinct natural beauty and attractions. Some parks are known for their iconic landmarks, such as the Grand Canyon in Arizona or Yellowstone in Wyoming. Others offer unique ecosystems, like the Everglades in Florida or Acadia in Maine. To make an informed choice, consider your interests, the time of year you plan to travel, and the type of experiences you seek. Research the parks' websites, guidebooks, and online resources to learn about their features, activities, and accessibility.

National parks have specific rules and regulations to protect their fragile ecosystems and ensure the safety of visitors. It's crucial to familiarize yourself with these regulations before your trip. Common park rules include restrictions on camping, campfires, and wildlife interactions. Additionally, some parks require permits for certain activities, such as backcountry hiking or fishing. Researching and adhering to park regulations will help you have a respectful and low-impact visit while avoiding potential fines.

Once you've chosen the national parks you wish to visit, it's time to plan your itinerary. Determine the duration of your trip and allocate time for each park accordingly. Remember that national parks can be vast, and exploring every corner in a single visit is often impossible. Prioritize each park's must-see attractions and activities and create a flexible schedule. Be sure to account for travel time between parks and consider overnight stays in campgrounds or RV parks along the way.

National parks offer a range of camping options, from developed campgrounds with RV hookups to backcountry camping for more adventurous travelers. If you plan to camp within the parks, making reservations well in advance, especially during peak seasons is essential. Some campgrounds offer full hookups for RVs, including water, electricity, and sewage disposal, while others provide more rustic settings with limited amenities. Research the available campgrounds, their facilities, and reservation procedures to secure your preferred accommodations.

Navigating your RV within national parks requires careful consideration of road conditions, size restrictions, and parking availability. While many parks accommodate RVs of various sizes, some roads may have length or height limitations, and parking spaces can be limited. Research each park's RV-friendly routes and roads to ensure a safe and stress-free journey. Pay attention to any advisories or closures that may affect your travel plans.

National parks experience different weather patterns and conditions throughout the year. Understanding the climate and seasonal variations is essential for planning your trip. Consider the average temperatures, precipitation, and daylight hours during your intended travel dates. Some parks may be best enjoyed during specific seasons, such as the vibrant fall foliage in Shenandoah National Park or the blooming wildflowers in Glacier National Park. Planning your visit during the right season can enhance your overall experience.

National parks are home to a diverse range of wildlife, and encountering animals in their natural habitat is one of the highlights of any RV trip. However, practicing responsible wildlife viewing from a safe distance is crucial to protect both you and the animals. Research the wildlife species present in the parks you plan to visit and learn about their behaviors and habitats. Follow park guidelines for wildlife viewing, which often include maintaining a minimum distance, not feeding animals, and securing your food to prevent wildlife encounters at campgrounds.

Safety should always be a top priority when exploring national parks. Familiarize yourself with park-specific safety guidelines, including hiking recommendations, water safety precautions, and first aid information. Having an emergency plan in place is also essential, including communication methods, emergency contacts, and knowledge of the nearest medical facilities. Carry essential safety equipment such as a first-aid kit, fire extinguisher, and tools for minor RV repairs.

National parks adhere to the Leave No Trace principles, which promote responsible outdoor ethics and environmental stewardship. These principles encourage practices such as packing out all trash, minimizing campfire impact, staying on designated trails, and respecting the natural environment. Embrace these principles to ensure that your RV trip has a minimal effect on the park's ecosystems and preserves its beauty for future generations.

National parks often have a rich cultural and historical heritage, with opportunities to engage with local communities and learn about the park's significance. Research any visitor centers, museums, or ranger-led programs that can enhance your understanding of the park's history, geology, and cultural heritage. Engaging with the park community and participating in educational programs can enrich your RV journey and provide a deeper connection to the natural surroundings.

Some national parks require permits for specific activities, such as backcountry camping, guided tours, or access to restricted areas. Research the permit requirements for the parks you plan to visit and make reservations as needed. Remember that permit availability can be limited, so early planning is essential to secure your desired activities.

In conclusion, researching national parks is a crucial step in planning a successful RV trip that allows you to fully enjoy these remarkable destinations' natural wonders and cultural heritage. You can ensure a safe, enjoyable, and memorable national park RV adventure by selecting the right parks, understanding park regulations, planning your itinerary, and considering factors such as camping accommodations, RV-friendly routes, and seasonal variations. Remember to practice responsible outdoor ethics, prioritize safety, and engage with the park community to make the most of your journey and create lasting memories in these cherished natural treasures.

Creating an itinerary

Embarking on an RV trip is an exciting adventure that promises the freedom to explore diverse landscapes, visit iconic destinations, and experience the joys of life on the open road. However, to make the most of your RV journey and ensure a smooth and enjoyable experience, creating a well-thought-out itinerary is essential. An RV trip itinerary is your road map, guiding you through your chosen destinations, activities, and accommodations. In this section, we will explore the key aspects of creating an itinerary for an RV trip, from planning your route and selecting campgrounds to allocating time for sightseeing and allowing flexibility for unexpected discoveries.

The foundation of any RV trip itinerary is the route you plan to take. Start by selecting your primary destinations, whether they are national parks, cities, scenic byways, or coastal routes. Consider the distance between each destination and the time it will take to travel between them. While it's tempting to pack in as many stops as possible, balancing exploration and relaxation is essential. Long drives can be tiring, so allocate sufficient time at each location to fully enjoy the experience. Research the roads, highways, and scenic routes that lead to your destinations, considering any size restrictions or road conditions that may affect your RV.

Once you have an outline of your route, it's time to select campgrounds and accommodations for your RV trip. Research campgrounds in advance and make reservations, especially if you plan to visit popular destinations or travel during peak seasons. Campgrounds vary in terms of amenities, hookups, and location, so consider your preferences and needs. Some campgrounds offer full RV hookups with water, electricity, and sewage disposal, while others provide more rustic settings with basic facilities. Think about the type of experience you want, whether it's a remote wilderness campground or a well-equipped RV resort with recreational amenities.

One of the joys of an RV trip is exploring the attractions and activities at each destination. Allocate time in your itinerary for sightseeing, outdoor adventures, and cultural experiences. Research the must-see attractions and activities at each stop and plan your days accordingly. Be realistic about how much you can do in a day, considering factors like travel time, the duration of activities, and the energy level of your travel companions. Some destinations may require multiple days to fully appreciate, while others can be explored in a few hours. Flexibility is key, as unexpected discoveries and spontaneous adventures often add depth to your journey.

While having a full and exciting itinerary is essential, it's equally important to plan for rest days. RV travel can be physically demanding, and taking a break to recharge is crucial for a pleasant and enjoyable trip. Designate rest days when you can relax at your campground, read a book, cook a leisurely meal, or simply enjoy the natural surroundings. Rest days also provide an opportunity for maintenance tasks, such as cleaning the RV and doing laundry. These breaks help prevent burnout and allow you to savor the experience without feeling rushed.

National parks, state parks, and natural landscapes offer a wealth of outdoor adventures, from hiking and biking to kayaking and wildlife viewing. Incorporate outdoor activities into your itinerary to fully immerse yourself in the natural beauty of each destination. Research the available trails, waterways, and guided tours in advance and plan your outdoor adventures accordingly. Be sure to pack appropriate gear and clothing for each activity, and consider your travel companions' fitness levels and interests when planning outdoor excursions.

Meal planning is an essential part of creating an RV trip itinerary. RVs come equipped with kitchens, making preparing meals on the road convenient. Plan your meals in advance by creating a menu and shopping for groceries before your trip. This not only saves time and money but also allows you to enjoy delicious home-cooked meals during your journey. However, don't forget to indulge in local cuisine and dining experiences at your destinations. Research local restaurants, food markets, and culinary specialties to savor the flavors of each region you visit.

While having a well-structured itinerary is essential for a successful RV trip, it's equally important to allow for flexibility. Unexpected opportunities and discoveries often arise during travel, and being open to change can lead to memorable experiences. Leave room in your schedule for spontaneous detours, unplanned stops, and serendipitous encounters. Flexibility also comes in handy when dealing with unforeseen challenges, such as inclement weather or road closures. Having a backup plan or alternate activities can help you adapt to changing circumstances and make the most of your journey.

Budgeting is a critical aspect of creating an RV trip itinerary. Calculate the expected costs of your journey, including fuel, campground fees, groceries, dining, activities, and any miscellaneous expenses. Set a daily or weekly budget to help you stay on track financially. It's also wise to carry a mix of payment methods, including cash, credit cards, and debit cards, to ensure financial flexibility during your trip. Keep track of your expenses and adjust your budget as needed to ensure you stay within your planned spending limits.

In today's digital age, staying connected while on the road is essential for safety and convenience. Research the availability of cell phone coverage and internet connectivity at your destinations. Some remote areas may have limited or no cell service, so plan accordingly. Consider investing in a mobile hotspot or satellite internet for reliable connectivity, especially if you need internet access for work or communication. Having a communication plan in place, including emergency contacts and a list of essential phone numbers, is crucial for peace of mind during your journey.

Safety should always be a top priority when creating an RV trip itinerary. Familiarize yourself with safety guidelines, including road safety, campground rules, and outdoor adventure precautions. Ensure that your RV is well-maintained and equipped with essential safety equipment, such as fire extinguishers, smoke detectors, and first-aid kits. Create an emergency plan that includes communication methods, the location of the nearest medical facilities, and procedures for handling unexpected situations. Share this plan with your travel companions to ensure everyone is prepared for any contingencies.

In conclusion, creating a well-planned itinerary is essential for a successful and enjoyable RV trip. It serves as your guide to exploring diverse destinations, allocating time for sightseeing, and ensuring a balance between adventure and relaxation. You can make the most of your RV journey by carefully planning your route, selecting campgrounds, allowing for rest days, incorporating outdoor adventures, and embracing flexibility. Remember to budget wisely, prioritize safety, and stay connected while on the road. A thoughtfully crafted itinerary sets the stage for a memorable RV adventure filled with exploration, discovery, and the freedom to roam the open road.

Reservations and permits

Planning an RV trip is an exciting endeavor that offers the freedom to explore diverse destinations and immerse oneself in the great outdoors. However, to ensure a smooth and enjoyable journey, navigating the world of reservations and permits is essential. RV travelers must be aware of the various reservations required for campgrounds, accommodations, and activities, as well as permits needed for specific experiences and locations. In this section, we will delve into the critical aspects of reservations and permits for an RV trip, emphasizing the importance of early planning, understanding park regulations, and maximizing the potential of your adventure while respecting the natural environment and preserving cherished destinations.

Securing campground accommodations is one of the first reservations to consider for your RV trip. Many popular RV campgrounds, particularly in national and state parks, fill up quickly, especially during peak seasons. It's crucial to plan ahead and make reservations well in advance to ensure you have a designated spot upon arrival. Research campgrounds that suit your travel route and preferences, considering factors like location, amenities, and hookups. While some campgrounds offer full RV hookups with water, electricity, and sewage disposal, others provide a more rustic camping experience with limited facilities. By reserving a campground spot, you guarantee a place to park your RV and access to necessary amenities.

If your RV journey includes national parks, be aware that each park may have its own reservation system and procedures. Some national parks, like Yosemite or Yellowstone, have high-demand campgrounds that require reservations made months in advance. Others offer a first-come, first-served system, where you secure a spot upon arrival. Researching the specific requirements and reservation policies for the national parks on your itinerary is crucial. Online reservation platforms and official park websites provide essential information about availability, reservation windows, and campground amenities.

For RV travelers seeking a more immersive outdoor experience, backcountry camping permits are often necessary. National parks and wilderness areas offer opportunities for venturing off the beaten path and spending nights in remote and pristine environments. However, backcountry camping typically requires a permit to regulate the number of visitors and protect fragile ecosystems. These permits may involve a reservation process and sometimes have associated fees. When planning an RV trip that includes backcountry camping, thoroughly research the permit requirements and reservation procedures for each park or area where you intend to explore. Remember that backcountry permits are often limited, so early planning is essential to secure your desired dates and routes.

Many RV travelers seek out unique activities and guided tours at their destinations. Popular activities such as guided hikes, boat tours, and wildlife encounters may require reservations due to limited capacity or seasonal availability. To avoid disappointment, research and book these activities in advance, especially if they are essential to your RV trip experience. Consider the interests and preferences of your travel companions when selecting activities, and be sure to check for any age or fitness requirements. Many national parks and recreational areas offer ranger-led programs that provide valuable insights into the natural and cultural history of the region, making reservations for such programs a worthwhile endeavor.

Some RV trips may include visits to restricted or protected areas within national parks or conservation areas. These areas often have special permit requirements to limit access and protect fragile ecosystems. Examples include areas with delicate desert landscapes, wildlife breeding grounds, or archaeological sites. Research the specific permit requirements and reservation procedures for any restricted areas you plan to visit. Special permits may involve guided access or limited entry during particular times, ensuring that these unique locations remain preserved for future generations to enjoy.

Campfire enthusiasts should be aware of fire permits and regulations in the areas they intend to visit. Many campgrounds and parks have restrictions on campfires, especially during dry seasons or in fire-prone regions.

Some locations may require a campfire permit to use a campfire ring or stove. These permits are typically easy to obtain and often involve a short briefing on fire safety. Ensure you are familiar with the fire regulations of your chosen destination and obtain the necessary permits to enjoy campfires responsibly.

RV travelers who enjoy fishing or hunting should be aware of state and federal regulations regarding these activities. Fishing and hunting permits and licenses may be required in certain areas, and bag limits and seasons vary by location. Research the specific rules and regulations for fishing and hunting in the regions you plan to visit. Ensure you obtain the necessary permits, follow catch and release guidelines if applicable, and always practice responsible and ethical angling and hunting practices.

As you plan your RV trip and make reservations or obtain permits, it's essential to adhere to Leave No Trace principles. These principles promote responsible outdoor ethics and environmental stewardship. They include practices such as packing out all trash, minimizing campfire impact, staying on designated trails, and respecting the natural environment. By following Leave No Trace principles, you contribute to preserving the natural beauty of the areas you visit and ensure that future generations can enjoy these destinations as well. While making reservations and obtaining permits is crucial for a successful RV trip, it's equally important to maintain a degree of flexibility and adaptability. Unexpected changes in weather, road conditions, or personal preferences can impact your travel plans. Having a backup plan or alternative activities can help you navigate these challenges. Additionally, staying open to spontaneous detours and unexpected discoveries can lead to some of the most memorable moments of your RV journey.

In conclusion, reservations and permits are essential components of planning a successful RV trip. They ensure you have a place to stay, access to activities, and the opportunity to responsibly explore protected or restricted areas. Early planning and thorough research are key to securing campground reservations, permits for backcountry camping, and reservations for activities and tours. By respecting park regulations and Leave No Trace principles, you can contribute to preserving natural environments and cultural heritage. Flexibility and adaptability are also vital, as they allow you to make the most of your RV adventure while embracing the spontaneity that often comes with travel. With proper planning and a commitment to responsible exploration, your RV trip can be a fulfilling and unforgettable experience.

CHAPTER IV

Packing and Preparing

Essential gear and supplies

Embarking on an RV trip is an adventure that promises the freedom to explore new destinations, enjoy the comforts of home on wheels, and create lasting memories with loved ones. However, it's crucial to be well-prepared with the right gear and supplies to make the most of your journey. Unlike traditional camping, where everything must fit in a backpack, RV travel allows for more extensive packing and the convenience of having many home comforts onboard. In this section, we will explore the essential gear and supplies you need for an RV trip, from safety equipment and kitchen essentials to outdoor gear and entertainment options, ensuring that you have a comfortable and enjoyable journey on the open road.

Safety should always be a top priority when embarking on an RV trip. Essential safety equipment includes fire extinguishers, smoke detectors, and carbon monoxide detectors. These devices can help protect you and your travel companions in case of emergencies. Additionally, a well-stocked first-aid kit is indispensable for treating minor injuries and ailments that may occur during your journey. It should include bandages, antiseptic wipes, pain relievers, tweezers, and any personal medications you may need.

RVs are like homes on wheels; just like any home, they may require occasional maintenance and repairs. A tool kit equipped with essential tools such as screwdrivers, pliers, wrenches, and a tire pressure gauge can be invaluable. Be sure to include spare fuses, light bulbs, and replacement parts specific to your RV model. Regular maintenance supplies like motor oil, coolant, and windshield washer fluid should also be on hand for routine checks.

RVs come equipped with kitchens, making preparing meals on the road convenient. To fully enjoy this aspect of RV travel, you'll need a well-stocked kitchen. Essential kitchen gear includes pots, pans, utensils, cutlery, plates, bowls, and cups. Don't forget kitchen appliances like a coffee maker, toaster, and microwave if your RV is equipped with them. A set of storage containers for leftovers and food preservation can be handy, as well as basic cleaning supplies such as dish soap, sponges, and trash bags.

Alongside kitchen essentials, you'll need a supply of cooking ingredients and supplies. Plan your meals and bring along the necessary groceries, spices, and condiments. Consider dietary restrictions and preferences when stocking your pantry. Non-perishable items like pasta, rice, canned goods, and dried herbs can be useful for creating various meals. If you plan to grill outdoors, be sure to bring a propane or charcoal grill and the associated fuel.

Comfortable sleeping arrangements are essential for a restful RV trip. Ensure you have enough bedding and linens for everyone on board. This includes sheets, pillows, blankets, and towels. If you're traveling during colder months, consider bringing extra blankets or sleeping bags for added warmth. Don't forget mattress covers and pillowcases for hygiene and comfort.

Pack appropriate clothing for the climate and activities you'll encounter on your RV trip. Layers are essential to accommodate changing weather conditions. Be sure to include outdoor gear such as hiking boots, rain jackets, and swimsuits if you plan to engage in specific activities.

Your packing list should also include personal items like toiletries, prescription medications, and any necessary travel documents (IDs, passports, insurance information).

RV travel often includes outdoor adventures, so having the right gear is crucial. Depending on your interests, this may include hiking boots, backpacks, bicycles, kayaks, fishing gear, or camping equipment. Research the activities you plan to pursue at your destinations and ensure you have the necessary gear and accessories to enjoy them fully.

While the journey itself can be entertaining, having additional options for leisure is essential during downtime. Consider bringing books, board games, playing cards, or electronic devices for entertainment. Many RVs are equipped with TVs and DVD players, so you can enjoy movies and TV shows while relaxing in the evening.

There are specific RV essentials that pertain to the operation and maintenance of your vehicle. These include items like leveling blocks to ensure your RV is parked on even ground, chocks to prevent it from rolling, and sewer hoses for emptying waste tanks at dump stations. Freshwater hoses and a water pressure regulator are necessary for connecting to campground water supplies. You should also have a supply of RV-specific toilet paper, as regular toilet paper can clog RV plumbing.

Enjoying the outdoor spaces at your campsite is one of the pleasures of RV travel. Bring along camping chairs and outdoor furniture to create a comfortable and inviting outdoor living area. These items allow you to relax outside, dine al fresco, and soak in the natural beauty of your surroundings.

Navigational tools such as GPS devices or navigation apps on your smartphone can be indispensable for finding your way to campgrounds and attractions. Additionally, consider having a backup map or atlas in case of technology failures. Communication equipment like a cell phone and, if necessary, a satellite phone or two-way radios can be crucial for staying connected and safe during your journey.

If you plan to stay at campgrounds or national parks frequently, consider investing in camping memberships or passes. Organizations like KOA (Kampgrounds of America) offer memberships that provide discounts and benefits at their campgrounds nationwide. National park passes like the America the Beautiful pass can grant you access to multiple national parks and federal recreational lands for a single fee.

In conclusion, being well-prepared with essential gear and supplies is fundamental to a successful and enjoyable RV trip. Safety equipment, maintenance tools, and kitchen essentials ensure your RV functions smoothly and that you can prepare meals comfortably. Bedding and personal items contribute to a comfortable living environment, while outdoor gear lets you make the most of your outdoor adventures. Entertainment options, RV essentials, and camping chairs add to your overall enjoyment, and navigation and communication tools enhance your safety and convenience. By packing thoughtfully and considering the specific needs of your RV trip, you can create a memorable and comfortable journey on the open road.

Safety tips for RV travel

RV travel offers the allure of the open road, the freedom to explore diverse landscapes, and the comfort of having a home on wheels. Whether you're a seasoned RV enthusiast or embarking on your first adventure, safety should always be a top priority. Traveling in an RV presents unique challenges and considerations, from the operation of a large vehicle to the potential hazards of campgrounds and unfamiliar roads. This section will explore essential safety tips for RV travel, encompassing aspects such as vehicle maintenance, safe driving practices, campground safety, fire safety, and personal security. By adhering to these guidelines, you can ensure a secure and enjoyable RV journey.

Regular maintenance is critical to the safe operation of your RV. Before each trip, perform a thorough inspection of your vehicle. Check the tires for proper inflation, tread wear, and signs of damage. Pay attention to the brakes, suspension, and steering components. Inspect the RV's engine, transmission, and fluid levels. Ensure that all lights and signals are functioning correctly. If you're not mechanically inclined, consider inspecting your RV by a professional before hitting the road. Proper maintenance helps prevent breakdowns and ensures that your vehicle is in optimal condition for travel.

An RV is different from a standard passenger vehicle due to its size and weight. Practice safe driving habits to minimize the risk of accidents and enhance your overall road safety. Allow for increased braking distance, especially when towing a trailer or driving a larger motorhome. Stay within speed limits, and avoid aggressive driving behaviors. Be mindful of blind spots, as RVs have larger blind spots than regular cars. Use your mirrors effectively, and consider installing additional safety mirrors if needed. Plan your route in advance, and be aware of height and weight restrictions on roads and bridges. Choose level and stable surfaces to prevent your RV from tipping or shifting when parking.

While campgrounds offer a sense of community and access to amenities, it's essential to prioritize safety within these environments. When parking your RV at a campground, ensure that it's level and stable to prevent accidents and discomfort inside the vehicle. Keep a safe distance between your RV and neighboring units to allow for fire safety and ease of movement. Be cautious when using campfires or grills, and follow campground rules and regulations regarding open flames. Keep an eye on children and pets to prevent accidents or wandering. Lock your RV when you're away, and store valuable items out of sight to deter theft.

Fire safety is paramount during RV travel, as the compact living space can exacerbate the spread of flames. Equip your RV with smoke detectors and carbon monoxide detectors, and test them regularly. Install fire extinguishers in easily accessible locations and know how to use them. Develop an evacuation plan for your RV in case of a fire, and ensure that all passengers are familiar with the exits and procedures. Avoid overloading electrical outlets, and keep flammable materials away from heating sources. Be cautious when using portable space heaters, and never leave them unattended. Additionally, always follow campground rules regarding campfires, firewood, and fire rings.

Personal security is vital to RV travel, especially when staying at campgrounds or boondocking in remote areas. Be aware of your surroundings and trust your instincts. Lock your RV doors and windows when you're inside or away from the vehicle. Consider installing additional security measures such as motion-activated lights or an alarm system. Keep valuable items secure and out of sight, and avoid displaying expensive equipment or belongings that may attract attention. When interacting with fellow campers or strangers, exercise caution and maintain personal boundaries. Establish a communication plan with your travel companions in case of emergencies or unexpected situations.

Weather conditions can change rapidly during an RV trip, so staying informed and prepared is essential. Monitor weather forecasts for your travel route and destination, and be aware of any severe weather alerts. Plan your travel schedule to avoid adverse weather conditions whenever possible. In the event of severe weather, seek shelter in your RV or a designated safe area and avoid driving until conditions improve. Carry emergency supplies such as flashlights, batteries, blankets, and non- perishable food and water in case you're stranded due to weather-related issues. Always have a backup power source for essential devices and communication.

Maintaining your health and wellness on the road is essential for a safe and enjoyable RV trip. Stay hydrated, eat nutritious meals, and get regular exercise to combat the physical demands of travel. Ensure you have an adequate supply of prescription medications and necessary medical supplies. Familiarize yourself with the locations of medical facilities and pharmacies along your route. Practice good hygiene and sanitation to prevent illness, and be vigilant about food safety when preparing meals in your RV kitchen.

Navigation and communication tools are indispensable for RV travel. Use GPS devices, navigation apps, or paper maps to plan your routes and find campgrounds and attractions. Stay connected with cell phones, and carry a backup power source or portable charger for your devices. Consider investing in a satellite phone or two-way radios in remote areas with limited cell coverage for communication and emergencies. Share your travel itinerary and contact information with trusted friends or family members, so they can reach you in case of unexpected situations.

Responsible RV travel includes minimizing your impact on the environment. Follow Leave No Trace principles by packing out all trash and waste, staying on designated trails, and respecting wildlife and natural habitats. Use environmentally friendly cleaning products and practices in your RV to reduce the release of harmful chemicals into the environment. Conserve water and energy by using these resources efficiently, and consider using solar panels or generators for off-grid camping to reduce your reliance on fossil fuels.

In conclusion, safety should always be a top priority when planning an RV trip. Vehicle maintenance, safe driving practices, campground safety, fire safety, personal security, weather preparedness, health and wellness, navigation, and environmental responsibility are all essential aspects of a safe and enjoyable RV journey. By following these safety tips and being prepared for various scenarios, you can experience the freedom and adventure of RV travel while ensuring the well-being of yourself, your travel companions, and the natural environment. RV travel offers the allure of the open road, the freedom to explore diverse landscapes, and the comfort of having a home on wheels. Whether you're a seasoned RV enthusiast or embarking on your first adventure, safety should always be a top priority. Traveling in an RV presents unique challenges and considerations, from the operation of a large vehicle to the potential hazards of campgrounds and unfamiliar roads. This essay will explore essential safety tips for RV travel, encompassing aspects such as vehicle maintenance, safe driving practices, campground safety, fire safety, and personal security. By adhering to these guidelines, you can ensure a secure and enjoyable RV journey.

Maintenance and RV checklists

Recreational vehicles, or RVs, have become increasingly popular for travelers seeking the freedom and flexibility to explore the open road. Whether you're a full-time RVer or just an occasional road tripper, ensuring the safety and functionality of your RV is paramount. Maintenance and RV checklists play a pivotal role in preserving the condition of your vehicle and ensuring a smooth journey.

In this section, we will delve into the importance of these checklists, explore the key components they encompass, and highlight the benefits they offer to RV enthusiasts.

To begin with, maintenance and RV checklists are fundamental tools for keeping your RV in top shape. RVs require regular maintenance to prevent breakdowns and extend their lifespan like any other vehicle. Neglecting this aspect can lead to costly repairs, unexpected inconveniences, and even safety hazards. Therefore, a comprehensive checklist that outlines the essential maintenance tasks is indispensable for RV owners.

A well-structured RV maintenance checklist typically covers various aspects of the vehicle, including the engine, electrical systems, plumbing, and exterior components. Regular engine maintenance ensures optimal performance and fuel efficiency, reducing the risk of engine-related issues during your travels. Inspecting the electrical systems helps prevent potential electrical failures that could leave you stranded or in the dark. Checking the plumbing ensures a reliable water supply for cooking, cleaning, and bathing, while addressing exterior components like tires, brakes, and seals safeguards against road accidents and leaks.

The process of creating and following an RV maintenance checklist is straightforward but requires diligence and organization. Firstly, you should consult your RV's owner's manual to identify specific maintenance requirements and schedules recommended by the manufacturer. This will serve as a foundational framework for your checklist. Additionally, you can seek advice from experienced RVers or professional mechanics to gather insights into common maintenance tasks and potential pitfalls.

Once you have gathered the necessary information, you can create a checklist tailored to your RV's make and model. This checklist should include regular tasks such as oil changes, air filter replacements, brake inspections, tire rotations, and fluid level checks. Moreover, it should consider seasonal considerations, like winterizing your RV to protect it from freezing temperatures or de-winterizing it when spring arrives. By adhering to your maintenance checklist, you can proactively address issues before they become significant problems, ultimately saving you time, money, and frustration.

In addition to maintenance, RV checklists are crucial in ensuring a safe and enjoyable journey. These checklists encompass a range of items to prepare you for life on the road, from packing essentials to safety precautions. A pre-trip checklist can help you avoid forgetting essential items and ensure you're adequately prepared for your adventure.

A pre-trip checklist typically includes items such as verifying your RV's overall condition, checking tire pressure, inspecting brakes and lights, and confirming that all appliances and systems are in working order. It also reminds you to stock up on necessary supplies, including food, water, toiletries, and camping gear. Moreover, it prompts you to check your route, confirm reservations at campgrounds or RV parks, and ensure that you have all the required documentation, such as driver's licenses and registration.

Safety should always be a paramount concern for RVers. Therefore, RV checklists emphasize safety measures, such as packing a well-stocked first-aid kit, having fire extinguishers readily accessible, and installing carbon monoxide detectors. Additionally, they remind you to practice safe driving habits, adhere to speed limits, and be cautious when towing or maneuvering your RV. Following these safety guidelines can minimize risks and ensure a secure and enjoyable journey for you and your fellow travelers.

Another crucial aspect of RV checklists is campground etiquette and environmental responsibility. These checklists remind you to respect the natural surroundings by disposing of waste properly, using designated campfire areas, and minimizing noise pollution. They also encourage you to be a considerate neighbor at campgrounds and RV parks, fostering a sense of community and goodwill among fellow travelers.

In conclusion, maintenance and RV checklists are indispensable tools for RV enthusiasts, whether they are experienced road warriors or newcomers to the RV lifestyle. Regular maintenance checklists help keep your RV in optimal condition, preventing breakdowns and costly repairs. Pre-trip checklists ensure you are well-prepared and safe on the road, reducing the risk of forgotten items or safety oversights. By diligently following these checklists, you can confidently embark on your RV adventures, knowing that your vehicle is reliable and your journey is planned to perfection. So, before you hit the open road, remember that a well-maintained RV and a comprehensive checklist are your keys to a safe and enjoyable adventure.

CHAPTER V

Life on the Road

Setting up camp

Recreational vehicle (RV) travel is a cherished mode of exploration and adventure for countless individuals and families. The allure of the open road, the freedom to explore diverse landscapes, and the comfort of having your own home on wheels are just a few of the reasons why RVing has become increasingly popular. However, to fully enjoy the RV experience, it's essential to master the art of setting up camp during your journey. This section will delve into the intricacies of setting up camp when you're on an RV trip, exploring the steps involved, the considerations to keep in mind, and the benefits of making your RV site feel like home.

The process of setting up camp in your RV involves several crucial steps that require attention to detail and organization. First and foremost, you must choose an appropriate campsite. Whether you opt for a campground, RV park, or a more remote boondocking location, it's essential to consider factors like availability, amenities, proximity to attractions, and your personal preferences. Reservations may be necessary for popular campgrounds, especially during peak travel seasons, so planning ahead is often advisable.

Once you've selected your campsite, it's time to navigate the RV into its designated spot. RVs come in various sizes and styles, so ensuring a smooth setup can be a challenge, especially for those new to RVing. Careful maneuvering, the assistance of a spotter, and clear communication between driver and guide are essential to avoid obstacles, prevent accidents, and position the RV correctly within the site. Leveling the RV is the next critical step, using leveling blocks or jacks to create a stable and even foundation.

With your RV properly situated, it's time to connect to utilities. Depending on the campsite, this may involve hooking up to electrical, water, and sewer systems. Ensuring a secure and functional connection to these utilities is crucial for a comfortable stay. Electrical hookups power your RV's appliances and systems, while water hookups provide a freshwater supply for cooking, cleaning, and bathing. Sewer hookups allow you to dispose of wastewater conveniently. Adhering to the correct sequence when connecting these utilities can prevent mishaps and ensure a trouble-free setup.

The exterior setup of your campsite also includes extending awnings and slide-outs if your RV is equipped with them. These features expand your living space and provide shade and protection from the elements. However, using them judiciously is essential, considering factors like wind, rain, and space limitations within the campsite.

As the exterior setup progresses, it's time to create your outdoor living area. Many RVers bring along folding chairs, tables, and outdoor rugs to transform their campsite into a comfortable and inviting space for relaxation and socializing. The choice of outdoor furniture and accessories depends on personal preferences and the available storage space in your RV.

Turning our attention to the interior of the RV, it's time to unpack and organize. RVs come equipped with various storage compartments and cabinets, each serving a specific purpose. Efficiently using these spaces is essential for maintaining order and making the most of your living quarters. Stowing away luggage, outdoor gear, and personal items in designated storage areas can free up valuable living space inside the RV.

Another aspect of interior setup involves arranging and securing items for travel. During transit, RVs can experience movement and vibrations that may cause items to shift or fall. To prevent damage and ensure safety, it's crucial to secure loose objects, close cabinet doors securely, and take precautions to protect fragile items.

Creating a comfortable and functional living space inside the RV is critical to the setup process. RV interiors are designed to maximize space while providing the essentials for daily life. This typically includes a kitchenette or galley area equipped with a stove, refrigerator, sink, and microwave, as well as a bathroom with toilet, sink, and shower facilities. Organizing your kitchen utensils, cookware, and groceries can help you easily prepare meals. Additionally, ensuring that your bathroom is stocked with essential toiletries and linens is critical for maintaining hygiene and convenience.

Setting up camp also involves personalizing your RV to make it feel like home. Many RVers bring along items such as bedding, pillows, and decorations to infuse their living space with warmth and personality. Family photos, artwork, and favorite books can create a sense of familiarity and comfort during your journey. Ultimately, the goal is to make your RV an inviting and cozy home away from home.

Safety is a paramount concern when setting up camp in your RV. This includes adhering to campground or RV park rules, respecting the environment, and following safety guidelines for activities like campfires and outdoor cooking. It's essential to be mindful of fire regulations, use designated fire pits or grilling areas, and properly extinguish fires before retiring for the night. Securing your RV and belongings can also deter theft and ensure a worry-free stay.

Setting up camp during an RV trip is not just a series of logistical tasks; it's a process that transforms your RV site into a comfortable and inviting home on wheels. This careful preparation and organization allow you to enjoy your surroundings fully, connect with nature, and make lasting memories with loved ones. The benefits of setting up camp thoughtfully are numerous, including the ability to relax and unwind in a familiar environment, the convenience of having all your essentials at your fingertips, and the opportunity to immerse yourself in the beauty of your chosen destination.

In conclusion, setting up camp during an RV trip is a multifaceted process that requires careful planning, organization, and attention to detail. From choosing the right campsite to connecting utilities, creating an outdoor living space, and personalizing your RV's interior, each step contributes to the overall experience of RV travel. The effort put into setting up camp pays off in the form of a comfortable and enjoyable journey, allowing you to savor the adventure of the open road while feeling at home in your mobile abode. So, as you embark on your next RV trip, remember that creating your home on wheels is not just a necessity but an art that enhances the joy of RVing.

Cooking in an RV kitchen

Recreational vehicle (RV) travel has gained immense popularity in recent years, offering individuals and families the freedom to explore the open road while enjoying the comforts of home. One of the defining features of RV living is the ability to prepare meals on the go, thanks to the convenience of an RV kitchen. While RV kitchens come in various sizes and configurations, they are designed to provide a functional space for cooking while you're on the road. In this section, we will delve into the art of cooking in an RV kitchen, exploring the challenges and advantages it offers, and sharing tips and tricks to make your culinary adventures in your mobile kitchen a delightful experience.

RV kitchens, also known as galley kitchens, vary in size and layout depending on the type and size of the RV. Class A motorhomes, for example, often feature spacious kitchens with full-sized appliances and ample counter space, akin to a traditional home kitchen. In contrast, smaller RVs, such as Class B or Class C models, may have compact kitchens requiring a more creative meal preparation approach. Regardless of the size, RV kitchens have essential appliances and fixtures, including stoves or cooktops, refrigerators, sinks, and storage spaces.

One of the primary challenges of cooking in an RV kitchen is the limited space. RVs are designed to be compact and efficient, which means that kitchen space is often at a premium. This limitation can make meal preparation and cooking a bit more challenging compared to the spacious kitchens found in brick-and-mortar homes. However, with careful planning and organization, you can overcome these challenges and create delicious meals in your RV kitchen.

Efficiency is key when cooking in an RV kitchen. To maximize the available space, keeping your kitchen well-organized is essential. Utilize storage compartments and cabinets strategically, ensuring that cookware, utensils, and ingredients are easily accessible. Consider using stackable or collapsible kitchen items to save space when they're not in use. Magnetic racks and hooks can be handy for storing utensils and small pots and pans on the walls, freeing up valuable counter space.

Meal planning plays a crucial role in RV cooking. Before embarking on your journey, create a menu for the duration of your trip. Opt for recipes that are simple to prepare and require minimal equipment. Consider prepping some ingredients at home, such as chopping vegetables or marinating meats, to streamline the cooking process in your RV kitchen. Additionally, stock up on pantry staples like pasta, canned goods, and spices to minimize the need for extensive grocery shopping during your travels.

Another challenge in RV cooking is the limited cooking appliances. RV stoves or cooktops are typically smaller than those found in conventional kitchens, with fewer burners. This limitation may require you to adapt your cooking techniques and choose recipes that can be prepared using a single burner. One-pot dishes, stir-fries, and sheet pan meals are excellent options for RV cooking as they are efficient and require minimal equipment. Additionally, consider using portable appliances such as toaster ovens, slow cookers, or electric griddles to expand your cooking capabilities in your RV kitchen. These appliances can be used both inside the RV and outdoors, providing versatility in meal preparation. Propane grills or portable campfire setups can also be a great addition for outdoor cooking experiences.

Water conservation is essential when it comes to meal cleanup in an RV kitchen. RVs have limited freshwater and wastewater storage tanks, so using water judiciously is crucial. Use paper plates and disposable utensils sparingly, as they can generate unnecessary waste. Opt for reusable, eco-friendly kitchenware whenever possible. To minimize water usage, scrape off food scraps into a trash bag before washing dishes, and consider using biodegradable cleaning products that are gentler on the environment.

Despite the challenges, cooking in an RV kitchen offers several advantages that can enhance your travel experience. One of the most significant benefits is the ability to enjoy home-cooked meals while on the road. RV kitchens enable you to control the quality and ingredients of your meals, catering to your dietary preferences and restrictions. This can be especially important for those with food allergies or specific dietary requirements.

Cooking in your RV kitchen also allows you to save money on dining expenses. Eating out at restaurants for every meal can quickly add up, making RV cooking a cost-effective alternative. By shopping for groceries and preparing your meals, you can stretch your travel budget further and allocate funds to other aspects of your journey.

Furthermore, RV cooking encourages creativity and culinary exploration. With limited resources, you may find yourself experimenting with new recipes and cooking techniques, expanding your culinary repertoire. Local farmers' markets and roadside stands can be excellent sources of fresh, seasonal ingredients that inspire your culinary creations.

Another advantage of RV cooking is the flexibility it offers. You can choose when and where to dine, tailoring your meal schedule to your travel itinerary. Whether you prefer a leisurely breakfast by a serene lake, a picnic lunch at a scenic overlook, or a cozy dinner inside your RV, the choice is yours.

To make your RV cooking experience even more enjoyable, consider the following tips:

1. Create a well-organized kitchen: Maximize storage space, label containers, and keep utensils and cookware within easy reach.

2. Plan your meals: Create a meal plan, prepare ingredients in advance, and pack a well-stocked pantry to minimize the need for extensive grocery shopping.

3. Simplify recipes: Choose recipes that require minimal equipment and can be prepared in one pot or on a single burner.

4. Embrace outdoor cooking: Take advantage of portable grills or campfire setups for cooking and grilling outdoors.

5. Practice water conservation: Use water-saving techniques when washing dishes and opt for reusable kitchenware.

In conclusion, cooking in an RV kitchen is integral to the RV lifestyle, offering a unique and rewarding culinary experience. While it may present some challenges due to limited space and resources, careful planning, organization, and creativity can turn your RV kitchen into a hub of delicious meals and memorable moments. The advantages of home-cooked meals, cost savings, flexibility, and the opportunity for culinary exploration make RV cooking a valuable skill for any RV enthusiast. So, as you embark on your next RV adventure, embrace the art of cooking in your mobile kitchen, and savor the joy of creating culinary delights on the open road.

Managing waste and utilities

Recreational vehicle (RV) travel is a popular way to explore the great outdoors, offering the freedom to roam while carrying the comforts of home. However, along with the convenience of RV living comes the responsibility of managing waste and utilities. Sustainable RVing involves minimizing environmental impact by carefully handling waste and optimizing resource use. This section will delve into the essential aspects of managing waste and utilities during an RV trip, exploring the challenges and solutions, and highlighting the importance of sustainability on the road.

Waste management in an RV is a critical aspect of responsible RVing. RVs have tanks for freshwater, gray water (wastewater from sinks and showers), and black water (sewage from toilets). Properly managing these tanks ensures a clean and hygienic living environment while minimizing environmental impact. To start, it's essential to understand the capacity of your RV's tanks and their limitations. Overfilling tanks can lead to unpleasant situations and potential damage to your RV's plumbing.

Freshwater conservation is the first step in responsible waste management. RVers should be mindful of water usage, using low-flow fixtures, taking shorter showers, and turning off taps when not in use. Collecting and using rainwater for non-potable purposes, such as flushing the toilet, can also help reduce freshwater consumption. Gray water management involves using environmentally friendly soaps and detergents, as well as using biodegradable cleaning products. These measures ensure that the gray water released into the environment has minimal impact on ecosystems. Some RV parks and campgrounds have designated gray water dumping areas, allowing for responsible disposal.

Managing black water, on the other hand, is a more sensitive task. RVers must use RV-specific toilet paper that breaks down easily and avoid flushing non-biodegradable items like feminine hygiene products or baby wipes. Properly maintaining and emptying the black water tank at designated dump stations or facilities is essential. Following established procedures and using appropriate safety gear when handling black water is crucial.

Aside from waste management, efficient utility use is a fundamental aspect of sustainable RVing. RVs typically have propane tanks for heating, cooking, and refrigeration, as well as electrical systems powered by batteries and generators. Making the most of these resources while minimizing energy consumption is key to a sustainable RV lifestyle.

Propane conservation is essential for extending your trips' duration and reducing environmental impact. RVers should regularly inspect their propane system for leaks, ensure proper ventilation when using propane appliances, and use propane-powered devices efficiently. This includes using a high-efficiency RV refrigerator and regulating indoor temperature to avoid excessive heating or cooling.

Electricity management involves optimizing battery usage and reducing reliance on generators when possible. Solar panels can be a valuable addition to RVs, harnessing the sun's energy to recharge batteries and power appliances. LED lighting is an energy-efficient alternative to traditional incandescent bulbs, reducing electricity consumption. RVers should also consider investing in energy-efficient appliances and using power-saving settings on devices.

Sustainability in RV travel extends beyond waste and utilities to encompass overall resource use. RVers can reduce their environmental footprint by adhering to the "leave no trace" principles, which emphasize minimizing impact on natural surroundings. This includes respecting wildlife, following designated trails, and properly disposing of trash and recyclables in designated containers.

Sustainable RVing also involves responsible consumption and waste reduction. RVers can minimize single-use plastics by carrying reusable water bottles, utensils, and food storage containers. Shopping locally and supporting farmers' markets reduces the carbon footprint associated with food transportation. Avoiding disposable items and choosing products with minimal packaging can further reduce waste generation during RV trips.

Water management is another aspect of sustainability during RV travel. RVers can conserve water by collecting and reusing gray water for outdoor purposes, such as watering plants or rinsing off outdoor gear. Installing low-flow fixtures and water-saving devices in the RV's plumbing system can also contribute to efficient water use.

Additionally, responsible disposal of waste and recycling materials is essential. RVers should be aware of local recycling programs and disposal regulations in the areas they visit. Many campgrounds and RV parks provide recycling bins and guidelines for waste separation. It's essential to follow these guidelines to reduce the environmental impact of your travels.

Furthermore, responsible camping practices include minimizing noise pollution, respecting quiet hours, and avoiding excessive use of generators, especially in natural and remote areas. Being considerate of fellow campers and the environment fosters a positive and sustainable RV community.

Sustainability during RV travel also extends to the choice of campsites and campgrounds. RVers can opt for eco-friendly campgrounds that prioritize environmental conservation and resource management. These campgrounds often have sustainable practices in place, such as energy-efficient lighting, water-saving measures, and recycling facilities.

In conclusion, managing waste and utilities during an RV trip is a practical necessity and a responsibility that aligns with sustainability principles. Proper waste management ensures a clean and hygienic living environment while minimizing environmental impact. Efficient utility use, including propane and electricity, reduces resource consumption and extends the duration of RV trips.

Sustainable RVing encompasses broader practices such as water conservation, responsible consumption, and minimizing environmental impact. By following "leave no trace" principles, minimizing single-use plastics, and supporting local businesses, RVers can reduce their environmental footprint. Choosing eco-friendly campgrounds that prioritize sustainability further contributes to responsible RV travel.

In embracing these principles and practices, RVers can enjoy the beauty of the great outdoors while preserving it for future generations. Sustainable RVing benefits the environment and enhances the overall RV experience, fostering a sense of responsibility, community, and respect for nature on the open road.

CHAPTER VI

Exploring National Parks

Highlighting top national parks for RVers

Recreational vehicle (RV) travel offers a unique way to explore the diverse and breathtaking landscapes of the United States. With the freedom to roam at your own pace and the convenience of having your home on wheels, RVers can visit some of the country's most iconic and stunning national parks. In this section, we will highlight a selection of top national parks that are especially well- suited for RVers, offering a range of natural wonders, outdoor activities, and RV-friendly facilities. From Yellowstone's rugged mountains to Zion's mesmerizing canyons, these national parks provide unforgettable experiences for those traveling in their RVs.

Yellowstone National Park, Wyoming, Montana, and Idaho

Yellowstone National Park, often called America's first national park, is a paradise for RVers and nature enthusiasts alike. Spanning across Wyoming, Montana, and Idaho, Yellowstone is renowned for its geothermal wonders, including the famous Old Faithful geyser. RVers can explore the park's diverse landscapes, from the bubbling mud pots of Norris Geyser Basin to the pristine lakes and lush forests of the Lamar Valley.

The park offers several RV-friendly campgrounds with various hook-up options, ensuring a comfortable stay. Yellowstone's extensive road network is perfect for RV travel, with scenic drives like the Grand Loop Road providing access to major attractions. Wildlife enthusiasts can spot bison, elk, grizzly bears, and wolves in their natural habitat. Hiking, fishing, and wildlife photography are just a few of the activities that make Yellowstone a must-visit destination for RVers.

Grand Canyon National Park, Arizona

The Grand Canyon, one of the world's most awe-inspiring natural wonders, beckons RVers to explore its vast depths and breathtaking vistas. With several RV-friendly campgrounds situated on the South and North Rims, visitors can enjoy the unparalleled experience of waking up to panoramic canyon views. Reservations are highly recommended, as campgrounds tend to fill up quickly, especially during peak seasons.

The South Rim, the park's most visited area, offers numerous viewpoints, hiking trails, and interpretive programs. RVers can embark on the Rim Trail, which offers accessible paths and stunning overlooks. For a more challenging adventure, hiking into the canyon or taking a mule ride can provide a deeper appreciation of the Grand Canyon's geological wonders. While less crowded, the North Rim offers equally spectacular views and a more serene atmosphere.

Zion National Park, Utah

Zion National Park, located in southern Utah, is a paradise for outdoor enthusiasts and RVers alike. The park's towering red rock formations, narrow slot canyons, and lush valleys make it a haven for hikers, climbers, and photographers. Zion's main canyon, Zion Canyon, is a must-visit destination with its stunning scenic drive and access to iconic trails like the Narrows and Angels Landing.

Several RV campgrounds are available inside and outside the park, with facilities catering to larger vehicles. During the peak season, making reservations well in advance is advisable, as Zion is a popular destination for RVers. The park operates a free shuttle system during busy months, making it easy to access trailheads and viewpoints without the hassle of driving your RV through crowded areas.

Yosemite National Park, California

Yosemite National Park in California is a land of towering granite cliffs, lush meadows, and cascading waterfalls. It's a dream destination for RVers seeking adventure and natural beauty. The park offers several campgrounds that can accommodate RVs, with hook-up options available in some areas. However, due to high demand, reservations are essential, especially during summer.

Yosemite Valley is the park's most iconic area, with world-famous landmarks like El Capitan, Half Dome, and Bridalveil Fall. RVers can explore the valley's hiking trails, take in the breathtaking scenery, and capture the beauty of Yosemite through photography. Tunnel View and Glacier Point provide panoramic vistas that are not to be missed. Beyond the valley, RVers can explore the High Sierra wilderness, including the Tuolumne Meadows and Mariposa Grove of Giant Sequoias.

Acadia National Park, Maine

Acadia National Park, located on Mount Desert Island in Maine, offers a unique coastal experience for RVers. With its rugged Atlantic coastline, granite peaks, and diverse ecosystems, Acadia provides hiking, biking, bird-watching opportunities, and more. Several RV-friendly campgrounds can accommodate larger vehicles, with facilities that cater to the needs of RV travelers.

The Park Loop Road provides access to many of Acadia's highlights, including Cadillac Mountain, Jordan Pond, and Sand Beach. RVers can enjoy scenic drives along the coastline and explore the park's extensive trail system. Additionally, the charming town of Bar Harbor, located adjacent to the park, offers dining, shopping, and cultural attractions that provide a well-rounded experience for RV travelers.

Great Smoky Mountains National Park, North Carolina and Tennessee

As the most visited national park in the United States, the Great Smoky Mountains National Park offers RVers a unique blend of natural beauty and cultural history. Straddling the border between North Carolina and Tennessee, this park is renowned for its mist-shrouded mountains, cascading waterfalls, and diverse flora and fauna.

RVers can choose from several campgrounds with RV sites, although hook-up options are limited within the park. Cades Cove is a popular destination for wildlife viewing and cycling, while Clingmans Dome offers panoramic views from the park's highest point. The Great Smoky Mountains also boast a rich cultural heritage, with historic buildings and interpretive programs that showcase the region's Appalachian history.

Rocky Mountain National Park, Colorado

Nestled in the heart of the Colorado Rockies, Rocky Mountain National Park beckons RVers with its alpine landscapes, pristine lakes, and abundant wildlife. The park offers several campgrounds with RV sites, but due to high demand, reservations are recommended, especially during the summer months.

Trail Ridge Road, one of the park's scenic drives, takes RVers to elevations above 12,000 feet, providing breathtaking views of the surrounding peaks and valleys. Hiking, wildlife watching, and photography are popular activities, with numerous trails and viewpoints to explore.

RVers can also visit the quaint town of Estes Park, located at the park's eastern entrance, for shopping, dining, and cultural attractions.

Bryce Canyon National Park, Utah

Bryce Canyon National Park, located in southern Utah, is famous for its otherworldly landscape of hoodoos—tall, slender rock spires that create a surreal and mesmerizing terrain. RVers can explore the park's scenic drive, which offers numerous overlooks and viewpoints to take in the stunning vistas.

The park provides RV-friendly campgrounds with varying amenities, making it possible to enjoy the unique camping experience amid the hoodoos. Bryce Canyon's clear night skies make it an excellent destination for stargazing and astrophotography. Hiking among the hoodoos on trails like the Queen's Garden or Navajo Loop Trail allows RV travelers to immerse themselves in this captivating landscape.

Arches National Park, Utah

Arches National Park in southeastern Utah is a geological wonderland, boasting over 2,000 natural sandstone arches. The park's unique rock formations, such as Delicate Arch and Landscape Arch, draw photographers, hikers, and adventurers worldwide.

While Arches National Park does not have RV campgrounds within the park itself, RVers can find suitable accommodations in the nearby town of Moab. The park is easily accessible by RV, and its scenic drive leads to many of the iconic arches and viewpoints. Hiking among the towering rock formations, capturing the play of light and shadows, and witnessing breathtaking sunsets are some of the highlights that make Arches a must-visit destination for RVers.

In conclusion, exploring the top national parks in the United States in an RV offers a unique and rewarding way to experience the country's natural wonders. From the geothermal wonders of Yellowstone to the awe-inspiring Grand Canyon, each national park has its own unique charm and attractions for RV travelers. Whether you seek the tranquility of Acadia's coast or the majesty of the Rocky Mountains, these national parks provide a wealth of outdoor adventures and memorable experiences for those traveling in their RVs. So, load up your RV, hit the road, and embark on an unforgettable journey to discover the beauty and wonder of America's national parks on wheels.

Must-see attractions in each park

America's national parks are a treasure trove of natural beauty and diverse landscapes, each offering unique attractions that draw millions of visitors annually. From the rugged wilderness of Alaska's Denali National Park to the iconic geysers of Yellowstone, these parks showcase the best of what the United States has to offer in terms of outdoor wonders. In this section, we will explore must-see attractions in a selection of these national parks, highlighting the iconic landmarks and natural wonders that make them beloved destinations for travelers and nature enthusiasts.

Yellowstone National Park, Wyoming, Montana, and Idaho

Yellowstone National Park, America's first national park, is a geological marvel and a wildlife sanctuary rolled into one. Among its must-see attractions is the world-famous Old Faithful geyser, which erupts approximately every 90 minutes, shooting a plume of scalding water and steam into the air. The geyser's predictable schedule makes it a favorite among park visitors.

Another iconic feature of Yellowstone is the Grand Canyon of the Yellowstone, a breathtaking chasm carved by the Yellowstone River. Its vibrant colors and cascading waterfalls, including the Lower Falls and Upper Falls, create a stunning visual spectacle.

The Mammoth Hot Springs, with its terraces of travertine formations, is another wonder that captivates visitors. These unique mineral deposits give the area an otherworldly appearance, and the ever-changing landscape continues to evolve over time.

Wildlife enthusiasts flock to Yellowstone for a chance to witness the park's abundant wildlife. Bison, elk, grizzly bears, and wolves roam freely in their natural habitat. The Lamar Valley, often referred to as the "Serengeti of North America," is a prime location for wildlife watching.

Grand Canyon National Park, Arizona

The Grand Canyon, one of Earth's most famous natural wonders, offers a breathtaking experience like no other. Visitors come from all over the world to witness the vastness of this immense canyon. Mather Point and Yavapai Point are popular viewpoints that provide awe-inspiring panoramas of the canyon's depths and the Colorado River below.

For those seeking a more adventurous experience, hiking into the canyon is a must. The South Kaibab Trail and Bright Angel Trail offer stunning perspectives as you descend into the heart of the Grand Canyon. However, it's essential to be well-prepared, as these hikes are physically demanding.

Havasu Falls, located in a remote corner of the Grand Canyon, is a hidden gem known for its turquoise waters and stunning waterfalls. The Havasupai Tribe oversees this area, and visitors need a permit to access it. The journey to Havasu Falls is an adventure in itself, as it involves a hike through the canyon and a stay in a rustic campground.

Zion National Park, Utah

Zion National Park is a landscape of towering red rock formations, narrow slot canyons, and lush valleys. The Zion Canyon Scenic Drive is a must-see attraction, offering access to several iconic landmarks. The Riverside Walk, a paved trail along the Virgin River, leads to the enchanting Narrows, where you can hike in the river itself.

Angels Landing is a famous hike that provides spectacular views of Zion Canyon. This strenuous trail involves navigating steep switchbacks and a narrow ridge with chains for assistance. The reward at the summit is a panoramic vista of the surrounding landscape.

The Subway, a unique slot canyon, is a challenging but rewarding hike for those seeking adventure. Permits are required, as the number of hikers is limited to preserve the fragile environment.

Yosemite National Park, California

Yosemite National Park is a landscape of towering granite cliffs, cascading waterfalls, and lush meadows. Yosemite Valley, with its iconic landmarks, is a must-see attraction. El Capitan, a massive granite monolith, is a world-renowned destination for rock climbers. The park's most famous waterfall, Yosemite Falls, is a captivating sight, especially in the spring when it is at its peak flow.

Half Dome, another iconic feature of Yosemite, offers a challenging but rewarding hike. The trail to the summit involves steep switchbacks and a climb up a cable route to reach the top. The panoramic view from Half Dome is a highlight for hikers.

Glacier Point, accessible by car or shuttle, provides one of the most breathtaking vistas in the park. Visitors can take in the panoramic views of Yosemite Valley, Half Dome, and the High Sierra peaks from this vantage point.

Mariposa Grove of Giant Sequoias is home to some of the world's largest and oldest trees, including the famous Grizzly Giant and the California Tunnel Tree. A visit to this grove is a journey into the ancient and awe-inspiring world of giant sequoias.

Acadia National Park, Maine

Acadia National Park, located on Mount Desert Island in Maine, offers a unique coastal experience. Cadillac Mountain, the highest point on the east coast of the United States, is a must-see attraction, especially for sunrise or sunset views. The Park Loop Road, which circles the island, provides access to many of the park's highlights.

Jordan Pond, with its crystal-clear waters and the iconic Jordan Pond House, is a favorite destination for picnics and leisurely walks. Visitors can also enjoy tea and popovers at the Jordan Pond House while taking in the serene surroundings.

Thunder Hole, a natural rock formation, creates a thunderous sound when waves crash into a narrow chasm. It's an exciting spectacle for those who visit during high tide.

Great Smoky Mountains National Park, North Carolina and Tennessee

The Great Smoky Mountains, known for their mist-shrouded peaks and diverse ecosystems, offer a range of attractions. Clingmans Dome, the highest point in the park, provides panoramic views of the surrounding mountains. A paved path leads to an observation tower at the summit, offering stunning vistas.

Cades Cove, a scenic valley surrounded by mountains, is a popular destination for wildlife viewing. Visitors often spot deer, black bears, and wild turkeys while driving the loop road.

The Roaring Fork Motor Nature Trail is a winding, one-way road that takes visitors through lush forests and past picturesque waterfalls. Rainbow Falls, one of the trail's highlights, is a beautiful sight, especially after a rainfall.

Rocky Mountain National Park, Colorado

Rocky Mountain National Park, nestled in the Colorado Rockies, offers visitors a chance to explore alpine landscapes, pristine lakes, and abundant wildlife. Trail Ridge Road, one of the park's scenic drives, takes visitors to elevations above 12,000 feet, providing breathtaking views of the surrounding peaks and valleys.

Bear Lake, a popular destination in the park, offers serene waters and easy hiking trails. It's a fantastic spot for a leisurely stroll or a reflective moment by the lake.

Dream Lake, nestled in the Tyndall Gorge, is known for its stunning reflections of Hallett Peak and Flattop Mountain. The hike to Dream Lake is relatively short but offers breathtaking scenery.

Wildlife enthusiasts can often spot elk, mule deer, and bighorn sheep throughout the park. The meadows around Moraine Park and the Beaver Meadows Visitor Center are excellent places to observe these animals.

Bryce Canyon National Park, Utah

Bryce Canyon National Park is renowned for its unique landscape of hoodoos—tall, slender rock spires that create a surreal and mesmerizing terrain. Sunrise Point and Sunset Point offer some of the most dramatic views of the amphitheater filled with hoodoos. The park's striking vistas make it an excellent location for photography.

The Navajo Loop Trail, which descends into the canyon among the hoodoos, is a popular hike. It provides an up-close experience with these unique rock formations. Queen's Garden Trail is another hike that offers a glimpse into the intricate world of Bryce Canyon.

Bryce Canyon is designated as an International Dark Sky Park, making it an exceptional location for stargazing. Visitors can marvel at a vast expanse of stars and celestial wonders on clear nights.

Arches National Park, Utah

Arches National Park, located in southeastern Utah, is a geological wonderland with over 2,000 natural sandstone arches. Delicate Arch, the park's most iconic feature, is a must-see attraction. The hike to Delicate Arch is moderately challenging but rewards hikers with an unobstructed view of this famous arch.

Landscape Arch, one of the longest natural arches in the world, is accessible via a relatively easy hike. The arch's slender form and delicate appearance make it a captivating sight.

Double Arch is a unique formation where two arches share a common base. It's an easy walk to reach this impressive double arch, making it accessible for visitors of all ages.

Balanced Rock, a massive sandstone boulder perched atop a slender pedestal, is another remarkable feature that captivates the imagination of visitors.

In conclusion, America's national parks are teeming with awe-inspiring attractions and natural wonders catering to various interests and outdoor pursuits. From the geothermal wonders of Yellowstone to the majestic vistas of the Grand Canyon, these parks offer iconic landmarks and breathtaking landscapes that continue to inspire and amaze visitors from all over the world. Whether you're a hiker, photographer, wildlife enthusiast, or simply someone seeking to connect with nature, the national parks of the United States provide an abundance of must-see attractions that make them cherished destinations for all who venture into their depths and beauty.

Hiking and outdoor activities

For many recreational vehicle (RV) enthusiasts, the allure of life on the open road is synonymous with a passion for outdoor adventure. RVers are drawn to the freedom of exploration, the joy of discovering new landscapes, and the thrill of immersing themselves in nature's wonders. One of the most fulfilling ways to embrace the great outdoors while RVing is by engaging in hiking and various outdoor activities. In this section, we will delve into the world of hiking and explore a range of outdoor pursuits that allow RVers to connect with nature, stay active, and create memorable experiences in some of the most scenic locations across the United States.

Hiking is a timeless and accessible outdoor activity that offers RVers the chance to get up close and personal with the natural world. Whether you're a seasoned hiker or a novice, national parks, forests, and wilderness areas across the country provide an array of trails suited to all levels of experience and fitness.

In national parks like Yosemite, Zion, and Acadia, you'll find well-maintained trails leading to awe-inspiring vistas, serene lakes, and cascading waterfalls. The Half Dome trail in Yosemite, the Angels Landing trail in Zion, and the Precipice Trail in Acadia are just a few examples of exhilarating hikes that reward adventurers with stunning views and a sense of accomplishment.

For those seeking a more challenging trek, consider tackling long-distance trails like the Appalachian Trail or the Pacific Crest Trail. While hiking the entire length of these trails may require months of dedication, RVers can choose to explore shorter segments that offer a taste of the epic journeys these trails represent. These trails wind through diverse landscapes, offering a deep connection to nature and a sense of solitude that can be hard to find elsewhere.

Outdoor enthusiasts often relish the opportunity to observe wildlife in its natural habitat, and many national parks and wildlife reserves offer ideal settings for wildlife viewing. RVers can spot various animals, from bison and elk in Yellowstone to moose and bears in Denali. Birdwatchers can marvel at the diverse avian species that call these parks home.

For a unique wildlife experience, consider taking guided tours or participating in ranger-led programs offered by national parks. These programs provide valuable insights into the park's ecosystems and enhance your chances of spotting elusive creatures. Remember to respect wildlife by observing from a safe distance and refraining from feeding or approaching them.

Camping is an integral part of the RV lifestyle and offers RVers the chance to immerse themselves fully in the outdoor experience. Most national parks and public lands have campgrounds with RV-friendly sites, making it convenient to stay close to the action. Whether you prefer the solitude of primitive camping or the amenities of developed campgrounds, there are options to suit all preferences.
Camping allows RVers to enjoy the tranquility of the natural world after the day's adventures. Roasting marshmallows over a campfire, stargazing under the vast night sky, and falling asleep to the sounds of the

wilderness are just a few of the magical moments that camping in RVs can provide.

Many RVers are avid anglers who relish the opportunity to cast a line in pristine lakes, rivers, and streams. National parks and forests often provide excellent fishing opportunities, with catch-and-release and catch-and-keep options available. Whether you prefer fly fishing for trout in a crystal-clear mountain stream or angling for bass in a serene lake, there are fishing destinations to suit your preferences.

Water activities like kayaking, canoeing, and paddleboarding are also popular among RVers. National parks' lakes, rivers, and coastal areas offer ideal settings for these pursuits. Exploring calm waters, gliding past scenic landscapes, and encountering wildlife from a waterborne perspective can be both relaxing and exhilarating.

Biking is a fantastic way to explore national parks and scenic areas while staying active. Many parks offer designated biking trails that range from leisurely rides through flat terrain to challenging mountain biking routes for adrenaline seekers. Biking allows RVers to cover more ground than hiking while still enjoying the sights, sounds, and scents of the outdoors.

The Cades Cove Loop Road in Great Smoky Mountains National Park and the Going-to-the-Sun Road in Glacier National Park are examples of routes where RVers can enjoy scenic bike rides. Biking also offers the advantage of being an eco-friendly mode of transportation that reduces the environmental impact compared to driving.

For the adventurous spirit, rock climbing presents an opportunity to conquer nature's vertical challenges. National parks like Joshua Tree, Rocky Mountain, and Yosemite offer world-renowned climbing destinations with routes for climbers of all skill levels.

Rock climbing can be physically demanding and mentally stimulating, rewarding participants with breathtaking views and a sense of accomplishment. While it requires specialized gear and training, it can be an unforgettable way to connect with the natural world.

Many RVers are passionate photographers who relish the opportunity to capture the beauty of the outdoors. National parks provide a wealth of subjects, from dramatic landscapes and majestic wildlife to vibrant flora and intricate details.

Photography allows RVers to document their outdoor adventures, create lasting memories, and share the splendor of the natural world with others. Sunrise and sunset photography, in particular, can yield stunning results as the changing light bathes landscapes in warm, golden hues.

For those with an interest in astronomy, stargazing in national parks can be an awe-inspiring experience. Many parks are designated as Dark Sky Parks, meaning they have minimal light pollution and offer exceptional visibility of the night sky.

Setting up a telescope or simply lying back to watch the stars can reveal a celestial tapestry of planets, constellations, and meteor showers. Bryce Canyon, Big Bend, and Great Basin National Parks are just a few examples of destinations renowned for their pristine night skies.

Winter RVing opens up a whole new world of outdoor activities. National parks like Rocky Mountain and Yellowstone transform into winter wonderlands with opportunities for snowshoeing, cross-country skiing, and snowmobiling.

Exploring national parks' quiet, snow-covered landscapes can be a serene and magical experience. RVers can take advantage of heated RVs and cozy evenings by the campfire to stay warm during winter adventures.

In conclusion, RVers have a world of outdoor activities at their fingertips, allowing them to immerse themselves in nature and create memorable experiences while on the road. Hiking, wildlife viewing, camping, fishing, and a host of other pursuits offer the chance to connect with the great outdoors in national parks and wilderness areas across the United States. Whether you're seeking adventure, relaxation, or a deeper connection with nature, these activities enable RVers to make the most of their travels and truly embrace the natural beauty surrounding them. So, load up your RV, hit the road, and embark on a journey of outdoor exploration that promises adventure, inspiration, and a lifelong appreciation for the wonders of the natural world.

CHAPTER VII

Connecting with Nature

Wildlife encounters

One of the most enchanting aspects of RV travel is the opportunity to immerse oneself in the natural world and encounter wildlife up close. The United States is home to diverse ecosystems and species, making it a prime destination for RVers seeking memorable wildlife encounters. From the majestic bison of Yellowstone National Park to the elusive manatees of Florida's Crystal River, these encounters offer a deeper connection to nature and the chance to witness the beauty and diversity of the animal kingdom. In this section, we will explore some of the top wildlife encounters for RVers, highlighting the national parks, wildlife refuges, and unique destinations where these experiences come to life.

Yellowstone National Park, often called America's Serengeti, is a wildlife enthusiast's dream come true. RVers flock to this iconic park for a chance to witness an array of animals in their natural habitat. Bison, often considered the symbol of the American West, are a common sight throughout the park. These massive creatures roam freely, often causing "bison jams" as visitors stop to admire their majesty.

Elk, with their impressive antlers, graze in meadows and along riverbanks. Visitors can often observe these elegant creatures during the rutting season, when males compete for the attention of females.

Grizzly bears and black bears can also be spotted in Yellowstone, though they tend to be more elusive. The park's Lamar Valley is a prime location for bear sightings, especially during the early morning and evening hours.

Reintroduced to the park in the 1990s, Wolves have made a remarkable comeback. The Lamar Valley is one of the best places to spot these apex predators, known for their intricate social dynamics and cooperative hunting behavior.

Yellowstone is also home to various bird species, including bald eagles, ospreys, and trumpeter swans. Birdwatchers will find plenty to see, especially around the park's numerous lakes and rivers.

Everglades National Park, often called the "River of Grass," is a unique and biodiverse ecosystem that allows RVers to explore a subtropical wilderness. This park is renowned for its resident American alligators, which can be spotted sunning themselves near waterways and along the Anhinga Trail. The Anhinga Trail, in particular, offers excellent opportunities for birdwatching, with wading birds, herons, and cormorants aplenty.

Manatees, also known as "sea cows," are a beloved resident of Florida's waterways. RVers can observe these gentle giants in Crystal River, where manatees gather in the warm waters of King Spring during the winter months. Snorkeling tours allow visitors to swim with manatees, providing a unique and memorable experience.

The Everglades are home to an array of bird species, making it a birder's paradise. Roseate spoonbills, wood storks, and white ibises are just a few of the species that can be observed wading in the shallow waters or soaring above the sawgrass prairies.

The elusive Florida panther, a critically endangered species, also calls the Everglades home. While spotting a panther is rare, the thrill of knowing you are in their habitat adds to the sense of adventure in this unique wilderness.

Denali National Park and Preserve, located in the heart of Alaska, offers RVers a chance to witness the splendor of the Arctic wilderness. At the park's center stands Denali, North America's highest peak, surrounded by tundra, boreal forests, and glacier-fed rivers.

One of Denali's most sought-after wildlife encounters is the chance to spot grizzly bears. These powerful creatures roam the park's landscapes, foraging for food in the tundra and along the riverbanks. The Toklat River area is known for its bear sightings.

Moose, the largest members of the deer family, are commonly seen in the park. RVers can spot moose in wetlands and along the park's many lakeshores, often foraging on aquatic plants.

Dall's sheep, with their striking white coats, inhabit the steep cliffs and rocky outcroppings of Denali. RVers can use binoculars or spotting scopes to observe these sure-footed creatures navigating the rugged terrain.

Caribou, also known as reindeer, are a symbol of the Arctic wilderness. They can often be seen on the park's tundra, especially during their annual migrations.

Golden eagles, peregrine falcons, and gyrfalcons are among the park's bird species, adding to the diversity of wildlife encounters.

Cape Hatteras National Seashore, located along North Carolina's Outer Banks, is a haven for beach-loving RVers and wildlife enthusiasts. The seashore is known for its extensive sandy beaches, rolling dunes, and dynamic barrier island ecosystems.

The park is a nesting ground for sea turtles, including loggerhead, green, and leatherback turtles. RVers visiting during nesting season can participate in nighttime sea turtle nest monitoring programs, guided by park rangers.

Birdwatchers will find a wealth of shorebirds, wading birds, and raptors along the seashore. The Cape Hatteras National Seashore is part of the North Carolina Birding Trail, and numerous birding hotspots are accessible to RVers.

The park is also known for its abundant marine life. Dolphin and whale-watching tours are available for those looking to spot these magnificent creatures in their natural habitat.

Katmai National Park and Preserve, located in southern Alaska, offers RVers a chance to observe one of nature's most spectacular wildlife events: the annual salmon run and the gathering of brown bears. The park's Brooks River is famous for its brown bear population, and visitors can witness these giants fishing for salmon in the river's rapids.

The park's bear viewing platforms provide a safe and immersive experience, allowing RVers to observe bears in their natural habitat. The peak of the salmon run, typically in July, offers the best chance to witness this incredible wildlife spectacle.

Katmai is also home to a variety of bird species, including bald eagles, peregrine falcons, and auklets. Birdwatchers will find ample opportunities to observe these species along the park's rugged coastline and in its pristine wilderness.

Custer State Park, nestled in the Black Hills of South Dakota, is known for its stunning landscapes and iconic wildlife. RVers flock to this park for a chance to witness one of the largest free-roaming bison herds in the United

States. The annual Buffalo Roundup, held in September, is a must-see event, allowing RVers to watch as cowboys and cowgirls round up the park's bison herd.

The park is also home to pronghorn antelope, bighorn sheep, and white-tailed deer. RVers can spot these animals while driving along the park's scenic wildlife loop road or hiking its picturesque trails.
Birdwatchers will find a variety of bird species in the park, including wild turkeys, bald eagles, and red-tailed hawks. The park's diverse ecosystems, from rolling prairies to pine-covered hills, provide a rich habitat for avian life.
Okefenokee National Wildlife Refuge, located on the border of Georgia and Florida, is a vast and mysterious wilderness of swamps, marshes, and blackwater rivers. RVers seeking an off-the-beaten-path wildlife encounter will find this refuge to be a hidden gem.

One of the refuge's main attractions is the opportunity to observe American alligators in their natural habitat. Boat tours and wildlife viewing platforms allow RVers to get up close to these impressive reptiles, as well as a variety of bird species and other wetland wildlife.

The Okefenokee Swamp is home to various birds, including the elusive and endangered red-cockaded woodpecker. Birdwatchers can explore the refuge's waterways and trails to spot these unique species.
The park's dark, tannin-stained waters also provide excellent stargazing opportunities, as the absence of light pollution makes for exceptional night sky viewing.

In conclusion, RV travel provides a unique opportunity for wildlife enthusiasts to connect with nature and experience unforgettable encounters with the animal kingdom. Whether you're observing grizzly bears in Denali, sea turtles in Cape Hatteras, or bison in Custer State Park, these wildlife encounters offer a deeper appreciation for the beauty and diversity of the natural world. As RVers hit the open road, they can embark on a journey of discovery, where every turn of the wheel brings them closer to the wonder of the wild.

Birdwatching and stargazing

Recreational vehicle (RV) enthusiasts embark on journeys across the country, seeking adventure, tranquility, and a deeper connection with nature. Two activities that perfectly complement the RV lifestyle are birdwatching and stargazing. Both pursuits offer unique opportunities to engage with the natural world while on the road, allowing RVers to create memorable experiences in diverse landscapes. In this section, we will explore the joys of birdwatching and stargazing for RVers, delving into the benefits, techniques, and the inherent sense of wonder that these activities provide.

Birdwatching, the practice of observing and identifying birds in their natural habitats, is a favored pastime among nature enthusiasts. RVers are uniquely positioned to take advantage of this hobby, as they often travel through various ecosystems and regions teeming with avian life. One of the critical benefits of birdwatching for RVers is its accessibility; all that is needed is a pair of binoculars, a field guide, and a keen eye. Whether you're parked in a remote wilderness area or a bustling RV park, birds are ubiquitous and can be found virtually anywhere. RVers can explore the diverse avian life across the country, from the majestic bald eagles of Alaska to the vibrant songbirds of the Appalachians. Birdwatching provides a sense of connection with the environment and an opportunity to appreciate the delicate balance of ecosystems that support these winged creatures.

Furthermore, birdwatching enhances the RV experience by encouraging a deeper appreciation for the outdoors. It encourages mindfulness, as RVers patiently observe and appreciate the subtleties of avian behavior, plumage, and song. It fosters a sense of curiosity, as RVers become amateur naturalists, eager to learn about the species they encounter. Birdwatching also promotes environmental stewardship, as RVers become more attuned to the conservation needs of the habitats they visit and the species they encounter. Through the simple act of watching birds, RVers become advocates for protecting our natural world.

For those interested in taking their birdwatching to the next level, RVers can seek out specific birding destinations and events. National wildlife refuges, state parks, and designated birding trails offer prime opportunities to observe a wide array of species in their natural habitats. Many RVers join birdwatching clubs and participate in bird counts and festivals, fostering a sense of community and camaraderie with fellow enthusiasts. These gatherings provide a platform for sharing knowledge and experiences, enhancing the enjoyment of birdwatching for RVers.

In addition to birdwatching, stargazing is another captivating activity that complements the RV lifestyle. The vast expanses of the night sky, free from light pollution, beckon RVers to explore the cosmos. Stargazing offers a profound sense of wonder and an opportunity to connect with the universe on a grand scale. RVers often find themselves in remote locations with clear, dark skies, making it the perfect setting for celestial observations.

The benefits of stargazing for RVers are multifaceted.

Firstly, it invites a sense of tranquility and introspection. Gazing up at a starry night sky from the comfort of an RV awakens a deep appreciation for the beauty and vastness of the universe. RVers often report profound awe and humility when contemplating the celestial wonders above. Stargazing can be a meditative and spiritual experience, allowing RVers to escape the hustle and bustle of daily life and connect with something larger than themselves.

Moreover, stargazing encourages a sense of curiosity and lifelong learning. RVers can delve into the study of astronomy, learning to identify constellations, planets, and celestial objects. Telescopes and binoculars open up new realms of exploration, allowing RVers to observe distant galaxies, nebulae, and even the moon's craters in stunning detail. Many RVers become passionate amateur astronomers, sharing their knowledge with fellow travelers and sparking interest in the night sky.

To enhance the stargazing experience, RVers can plan their travels around celestial events such as meteor showers, eclipses, and planetary alignments. National parks and designated dark-sky preserves offer ideal settings for stargazing, where the absence of artificial light allows for unparalleled views of the night sky. Some RVers even incorporate astrophotography into their journeys, capturing breathtaking images of the cosmos to cherish as souvenirs of their adventures.

In conclusion, birdwatching and stargazing are two enriching activities that perfectly complement the RV lifestyle. They offer RVers the opportunity to connect with nature, cultivate mindfulness, and foster a sense of wonder. Birdwatching allows RVers to appreciate the avian diversity across the country while promoting environmental awareness. Stargazing, on the other hand, invites RVers to explore the cosmos, fostering a sense of awe and curiosity about the universe. Both pursuits enhance the RV experience, creating lasting memories and a deeper connection with the natural world. So, next time you hit the open road in your RV, don't forget to pack your binoculars and telescope, for the wonders of birdwatching and stargazing await you under the vast skies of our beautiful planet.

Sustainability and responsible camping

Recreational Vehicle (RV) travel offers a unique and adventurous way to explore the great outdoors while enjoying the comforts of home on the road. However, with the increasing popularity of RVing, the impact on the environment has become a concern. Sustainability and responsible camping have thus emerged as essential principles for RVers to embrace. In this section, we will delve into the importance of sustainability and responsible camping practices for RVers, exploring ways to minimize their ecological footprint and preserve the natural beauty of the destinations they visit.

One of the fundamental principles of responsible camping for RVers is Leave No Trace (LNT). This ethic emphasizes the importance of leaving the environment as pristine as it was found. RVers can follow LNT principles by disposing of waste properly, packing out all trash, and refraining from disturbing wildlife or natural features. RVs come equipped with waste disposal systems, including holding tanks for greywater and blackwater. Properly managing these tanks and disposing of waste in designated facilities is essential to prevent contamination of the environment. RVers should also carry trash bags and recycling bins, ensuring that all waste is properly contained and disposed of at appropriate locations.

Additionally, responsible camping entails choosing campsites wisely. Many campgrounds and RV parks offer designated sites with hookups for water, electricity, and sewage disposal. Opting for these sites reduces the strain on the environment, as these facilities are equipped to handle RV needs efficiently. When boondocking or camping in remote areas without amenities, RVers should be mindful of their impact. They can minimize their environmental footprint by selecting established campsites, avoiding fragile ecosystems, and staying within established boundaries. It's crucial to respect any posted regulations and guidelines to protect the delicate balance of nature.

Sustainability also extends to resource management while RVing. RVers can conserve water and energy by adopting eco-friendly practices. Installing low-flow faucets and showerheads, as well as using water-saving appliances, can significantly reduce water consumption. Solar panels and energy-efficient appliances can help RVers reduce their reliance on fossil fuels and minimize their carbon footprint. Properly maintaining and servicing the RV's systems can ensure that they operate efficiently and minimize resource wastage.

When it comes to transportation, RVers can practice sustainability by reducing their carbon emissions. Planning routes efficiently and avoiding unnecessary detours can help conserve fuel. RVers can also carpool or use alternative transportation methods, such as bicycles or public transit, to explore nearby destinations once they've parked their RV. Adopting fuel-efficient driving practices, like maintaining a steady speed and properly inflating tires, can further reduce fuel consumption.

Furthermore, responsible camping involves a commitment to preserving natural ecosystems and protecting wildlife. RVers should avoid disturbing wildlife by observing animals from a distance and refraining from feeding them. Feeding wildlife can disrupt their natural behaviors and diets, leading to ecological imbalances. It's essential to follow all local regulations regarding interactions with wildlife, as these guidelines are designed to protect both the animals and campers.

Invasive species can pose a significant threat to natural environments. RVers can unknowingly transport invasive species from one location to another. To prevent the spread of invasive species, RVers should thoroughly clean their RV and equipment before moving to a new area. This includes cleaning off mud, debris, and any plant matter that may harbor invasive species. Following these practices helps protect the native flora and fauna of each destination and ensures that the ecosystem remains intact for future generations of RVers to enjoy.

Sustainable and responsible camping also extends to RV travel's cultural and social aspects. RVers should be respectful and considerate of local communities and their customs. Engaging with local businesses, buying local products, and respecting the privacy and property of residents contribute to positive interactions between RVers and local communities. Moreover, practicing responsible camping etiquette, such as keeping noise levels down during quiet hours and adhering to campground rules, fosters a sense of community and mutual respect among RV enthusiasts.

Responsible camping also involves the principle of "pack it in, pack it out." RVers should carry all necessary supplies and provisions with them and avoid overconsumption. Minimizing waste and reducing reliance on disposable products can help RVers leave a smaller ecological footprint. Using reusable containers, bottles, and utensils, as well as opting for eco-friendly cleaning products, can significantly reduce the generation of single-use plastics and chemicals that can harm the environment.

In conclusion, sustainability and responsible camping practices are essential for RVers to minimize their environmental impact and promote natural beauty preservation for future generations. By adhering to Leave No Trace principles, conserving resources, practicing responsible wildlife interaction, and respecting local communities, RVers can enjoy the RV lifestyle while ensuring that the places they visit remain pristine and unspoiled. The responsibility lies with each RVer to embrace these principles and contribute to RV travel's sustainable and responsible future. Ultimately, by adopting these practices, RVers can continue to enjoy the beauty of nature while safeguarding it for years to come.

CHAPTER VIII

RV Communities and Resources

RV clubs and online communities

RVing offers a unique lifestyle combining adventure, freedom, and a sense of community. As RV enthusiasts traverse the open road, they often seek ways to connect with like-minded individuals, share experiences, and access valuable resources. RV clubs and online communities have emerged as powerful platforms that cater to these needs. In this section, we will explore the significance of RV clubs and online communities, their benefits, and the sense of camaraderie they provide to those who embark on the RV journey.

RV clubs have long been a cornerstone of the RVing experience. These clubs are typically organized by region, interest, or specific RV brands, catering to various preferences and lifestyles. Joining an RV club can be a transformative experience for RVers, as it instantly connects them to a supportive network of individuals who share their passion for RV travel. These clubs often organize rallies, events, and educational seminars, allowing members to come together and forge lasting friendships.

One of the primary benefits of RV clubs is the wealth of knowledge and expertise they offer to their members. Novice RVers can tap into the collective wisdom of experienced club members, learning about essential topics such as RV maintenance, trip planning, and safety. RV clubs frequently publish newsletters or magazines filled with valuable tips, advice, and travel stories, keeping members informed and inspired. This exchange of information is invaluable for those who are new to the RV lifestyle or seeking to enhance their RVing skills.

Moreover, RV clubs often negotiate discounts and special offers with campgrounds, RV parks, and suppliers, providing members with cost-effective solutions for their RV adventures. These perks can result in substantial savings on campsite fees, RV accessories, and even insurance rates. Joining an RV club can quickly offset its membership fees through these financial benefits, making it a wise investment for RVers who hit the road frequently. Another crucial aspect of RV clubs is the sense of community and belonging they offer. RVers joining these clubs become part of a tight-knit group with a common bond. This sense of camaraderie extends beyond the road, as members often gather for rallies and events throughout the year. These gatherings allow RVers to socialize, swap stories, and build lasting friendships. The RV lifestyle can sometimes be isolating, given the constant movement, but RV clubs create a sense of connection and support that helps combat loneliness and fosters a feeling of home on the road.

While RV clubs have long been a staple of the RV community, the digital age has ushered in a new era of connectivity through online communities. Online forums, social media groups, and websites dedicated to RVing have become virtual hubs where RV enthusiasts can connect, share, and learn from one another. These online communities offer several distinct advantages for RVers.

One of the primary benefits of online communities is their accessibility. RVers can access these resources from the comfort of their RVs, whether parked at a campsite or on the move. This accessibility allows RVers to stay connected and engaged with the RV community even when they are physically isolated. It is also valuable for obtaining real-time information, advice, and recommendations.

Online communities are a treasure trove of information, with members freely sharing their experiences, challenges, and solutions. Whether a RVer is troubleshooting a technical issue, seeking campground recommendations, or planning a cross-country trip, they can turn to these digital platforms for insights and guidance. The collective knowledge of online communities often rivals that of traditional RV clubs, making them indispensable for novice and seasoned RVers.

Furthermore, online communities are diverse and inclusive, accommodating RVers of all backgrounds, interests, and demographics. RVing is not a one-size-fits-all endeavor, and online platforms reflect this diversity by catering to various niches within the RVing community. Whether someone is interested in full-time RVing, boondocking, luxury RV resorts, or vintage trailer restoration, they can find an online community that aligns with their specific interests.

Online communities also facilitate real-time interactions and support. RVers can engage in discussions, ask questions, and seek advice from the comfort of their digital devices. Online communities offer a lifeline of assistance and guidance when challenges arise on the road, such as mechanical issues or emergency situations. RVers often report feeling a sense of camaraderie with online peers, even though they may never meet in person.

In recent years, social media platforms have played a significant role in connecting RVers online. Facebook groups, in particular, have become popular gathering places for RV enthusiasts. These groups cater to various aspects of RVing, such as specific RV brands, travel destinations, and lifestyle choices. Members of these groups engage in vibrant discussions, share photos and videos of their travels, and offer advice and support to fellow RVers.

In conclusion, RV clubs and online communities have become integral components of the RVing experience. They offer RVers a sense of belonging, a wealth of knowledge, and a platform for connecting with like-minded individuals. Whether through traditional RV clubs or digital online communities, RV enthusiasts can tap into a rich network of resources, camaraderie, and support as they embark on their RV journeys. These communities enhance the RV lifestyle and reinforce the idea that, no matter where the road leads, RVers are never truly alone on their adventures.

Finding RV-friendly campgrounds

For many recreational vehicle (RV) enthusiasts, the road less traveled is the path to adventure, freedom, and discovery. The appeal of RVing lies in the ability to explore diverse landscapes, soak in the beauty of nature, and experience the joy of life on the open road. However, the success of an RV journey often hinges on one critical factor: finding RV-friendly campgrounds. In this section, we will delve into the importance of locating the right campgrounds for RVers, share strategies for discovering RV-friendly options, and highlight the factors that make a campground truly accommodating to the RV lifestyle.

The significance of finding RV-friendly campgrounds cannot be overstated. Unlike traditional vacationers who may stay in hotels or resorts, RVers carry their accommodations with them, making the choice of campground a pivotal decision. The ideal campground should provide the essential amenities, comfort, and convenience that RVers require while also offering a connection to nature and the outdoors. After all, RVing is not just about the destination; it's about the journey and the experience along the way.

One of the primary considerations for RVers when selecting a campground is the availability of suitable RV sites. RV-friendly campgrounds typically offer designated RV sites that accommodate various sizes of RVs, from compact trailers to large motorhomes. These sites should be spacious enough to comfortably accommodate the RV, tow vehicle, and any slide-outs or awnings. Additionally, the sites should have level surfaces to ensure stability and ease of setup. Access to full hookups, including water, electricity, and sewage connections, is also essential for the convenience of RVers.

Another critical aspect of an RV-friendly campground is the availability of amenities and facilities that enhance the RVing experience. Campgrounds that offer clean and well-maintained restrooms, showers, and laundry facilities are highly desirable, as they provide RVers with the comforts of home while on the road. Campgrounds with on-site stores or supply shops can conveniently replenish essential supplies and groceries.

In recent years, the demand for connectivity has become increasingly crucial for RVers. Many RVers rely on the internet for work, communication, and entertainment while on the road. As such, RV-friendly campgrounds should offer reliable Wi-Fi or cellular reception, allowing RVers to stay connected with the outside world when necessary.

Furthermore, a campground's natural surroundings and ambiance play a significant role in the overall RVing experience. RVers often seek campgrounds that provide a sense of immersion in nature, with hiking, wildlife viewing, and outdoor recreation opportunities. Access to scenic views, tranquil lakes, or wooded trails adds to the appeal of a campground, allowing RVers to connect with the beauty of the natural world.

While the amenities and facilities are crucial, another aspect that RVers often consider is the campground's location and proximity to attractions and points of interest. RVing is about exploration, and RV-friendly campgrounds that are situated near national parks, historic sites, cultural landmarks, or outdoor adventures offer RVers the opportunity to explore their surroundings easily.

So, how do RVers go about finding these ideal campgrounds that cater to their needs and preferences? The answer lies in a combination of research, planning, and utilizing the available resources.

One of the most reliable resources for finding RV-friendly campgrounds is the internet. Countless websites and apps are dedicated to RV camping and provide comprehensive listings of campgrounds, complete with detailed information, user reviews, and photos. Websites like Campendium, RV Park Reviews, and RV Trip Wizard are valuable tools for RVers seeking campground information and recommendations. These platforms allow RVers to filter their search based on criteria such as location, amenities, and site size, making it easier to find campgrounds that align with their specific requirements.

In addition to online resources, RVers can turn to RV club memberships for campground recommendations and discounts. Many RV clubs, such as Good Sam Club, Escapees RV Club, and Thousand Trails, offer affiliated campgrounds directories that offer club members special rates and benefits. These directories often provide valuable insights into the quality and amenities of each campground, making it easier for RVers to make informed choices.

Social media and online forums are valuable sources of campground recommendations and real-world experiences. RVers can join online communities and social media groups dedicated to RVing to seek advice, share their campground discoveries, and connect with fellow RV enthusiasts. These platforms provide a sense of community and a wealth of firsthand knowledge that can be invaluable in planning an RV trip.

While the internet is a powerful tool for finding RV-friendly campgrounds, it's essential for RVers to exercise discernment and rely on multiple sources of information. User reviews and recommendations can vary, so it's advisable to cross-reference information from different platforms and consult reliable sources to ensure the accuracy of the information.

Planning ahead is another key aspect of finding the right campgrounds for RVers. RV travel often involves mapping out an itinerary and making early reservations, especially during peak travel seasons. Popular campgrounds near sought-after destinations can fill up quickly, so RVers should plan their routes, identify suitable campgrounds along the way, and secure reservations as early as possible to avoid disappointment.

Furthermore, flexibility can be an asset when searching for RV-friendly campgrounds. Some RVers prefer the spontaneity of traveling without reservations and are open to discovering campgrounds on the fly. While this approach can lead to serendipitous discoveries, it also carries the risk of limited availability during peak times. Flexibility is a personal preference, and RVers should choose the approach that aligns with their comfort level and travel style.

In conclusion, finding RV-friendly campgrounds is a crucial aspect of the RVing experience, as it directly impacts the journey's comfort, convenience, and enjoyment. RVers seeking the ideal campgrounds should prioritize factors such as suitable RV sites, essential amenities, natural surroundings, and proximity to attractions. Utilizing online resources, RV club memberships, and the wisdom of the RVing community can guide RVers in their quest to discover the perfect campgrounds for their adventures. Whether through meticulous planning or serendipitous exploration, RVers can embark on memorable journeys and create lasting memories by choosing campgrounds that align with their preferences and needs. Ultimately, the search for the perfect RV-friendly campground is an integral part of the RV lifestyle, offering RVers the freedom to roam and the joy of discovering new horizons.

Budgeting for your trip

Recreational vehicle (RV) travel offers the allure of adventure, exploration, and the freedom to roam at your own pace. Whether you're planning a short weekend getaway or an extended cross-country journey, effective budgeting is crucial to ensure that your RV trip is both enjoyable and financially sustainable. In this section, we will delve into the importance of budgeting for your RV trip, discuss critical factors to consider, and provide practical tips for managing your finances while on the road.

The significance of budgeting for your RV trip cannot be overstated. RVing offers a unique travel experience, combining transportation and accommodation into one unit. While it can be a cost-effective way to explore new destinations, the expenses associated with RV travel can vary significantly depending on your preferences, travel style, and chosen destinations. Effective budgeting allows you to plan your trip confidently, make informed decisions, and ensure that you stay within your financial means.

Before embarking on your RV adventure, assessing your financial situation and setting a realistic budget is essential. Start by calculating your total trip budget, considering all anticipated expenses. This should include costs such as fuel, campsite fees, food, entertainment, RV maintenance, insurance, and any other expenses specific to your trip. It's advisable to overestimate your expenses slightly to accommodate unexpected costs and emergencies.

The largest expense for RVers is typically fuel, as RVs are not known for their fuel efficiency. To estimate your fuel costs, consider the distance you plan to travel, the average miles per gallon (MPG) of your RV, and the current price of fuel. By factoring in these variables, online tools and apps can help you calculate fuel costs more accurately. Remember that fuel prices can fluctuate, so it's a good practice to check for current prices and plan your route accordingly.

Campsite fees are another significant expense for RVers. Campgrounds offer a range of options, from basic sites with minimal amenities to luxury resorts with full hookups and recreational facilities. The cost of campsites can vary widely, with more desirable locations often commanding higher fees. It's crucial to research campgrounds in advance, compare rates, and make reservations when necessary, especially during peak travel seasons. Some RVers choose to mix in free or low-cost boondocking (dry camping) options to reduce campsite expenses, but it's essential to carefully research and plan for these options.

Food expenses are a variable cost that can be managed through smart planning and budgeting. RVers can cook their meals in the onboard kitchen, dine out, or combine both. Meal planning, buying groceries in bulk, and using local markets can help stretch your food budget. Budgeting for occasional dining out or trying local cuisine as part of the travel experience is also a good idea.

Entertainment and activities can add enjoyment to your RV trip but can also be a significant expense if not managed wisely. Consider the cost of admission to attractions, museums, national parks, and any planned activities or excursions. Look for discounts, passes, or memberships that can help reduce these costs. Additionally, seek out free or low-cost recreational opportunities, such as hiking, biking, and exploring natural wonders, to balance your entertainment budget.

RV maintenance is a crucial aspect of budgeting that should not be overlooked. While RVs are designed for durability and reliability, they require routine maintenance to ensure safe and trouble-free travel. Budget for regular oil changes, tire inspections, and other preventive measures. It's also wise to set aside funds for unexpected repairs or emergencies, as breakdowns can happen, and having financial reserves for such situations is essential for peace of mind.

Insurance is another essential expense for RVers. RV insurance coverage can vary depending on the type of RV, its value, and your specific needs. Shop around for insurance quotes, and be sure to understand your policy's coverage and deductibles. Having adequate insurance is essential for protecting your investment and providing financial security in case of accidents or unforeseen events.

In addition to these primary expenses, it's essential to budget for miscellaneous costs that may arise during your RV trip. These can include laundry expenses, tolls, vehicle registration fees, propane for cooking and heating, and other incidentals. Having a dedicated fund for these miscellaneous expenses ensures that you have the flexibility to address unexpected financial needs without disrupting your overall budget.

While budgeting for your RV trip is essential for managing expenses, monitoring and tracking your spending as you travel is equally important. Keeping a detailed record of your expenses, whether through a budgeting app or a simple spreadsheet, allows you to stay accountable to your budget and make adjustments as needed. Regularly reviewing your spending can also help you identify areas where you can save money or allocate funds more efficiently.

As you travel, consider adopting cost-saving strategies to maximize your budget. For example, taking advantage of campground memberships or loyalty programs can lead to discounts on campsite fees. Many RVers also explore workamping or volunteer camping opportunities, where they exchange labor or services for free or reduced campsite fees. Additionally, minimizing unnecessary purchases and practicing frugality can help stretch your budget and make your RV trip more financially sustainable.

Building an emergency fund is another essential aspect of budgeting for your RV trip. Unexpected expenses or emergencies, such as medical bills, vehicle repairs, or unforeseen circumstances, can arise anytime. Having a financial cushion in the form of an emergency fund provides peace of mind and financial security. Experts often recommend setting aside three to six months' worth of living expenses in your emergency fund.

In conclusion, budgeting for your RV trip is fundamental to ensuring a successful and financially sustainable journey. By assessing your financial situation, setting a realistic budget, and monitoring your expenses while on the road, you can enjoy the freedom and adventure of RV travel without the stress of financial uncertainty. Effective budgeting empowers you to make informed decisions, prioritize your spending, and confidently navigate the open road. With careful planning and financial discipline, your RV trip can be a roadmap to financial freedom, where you can savor the thrill of the journey while staying within your means.

CHAPTER IX

Challenges and Solutions

Dealing with RV breakdowns

Recreational vehicle (RV) travel is an exhilarating pursuit that offers the freedom to explore new horizons and embrace the open road. However, the road can be unpredictable, and RV breakdowns are an unfortunate reality that RVers may encounter during their journeys. Dealing with RV breakdowns is essential for any RV enthusiast, as it can mean the difference between a minor inconvenience and a major crisis. In this section, we will explore the importance of being prepared for RV breakdowns, discuss common causes of breakdowns, and provide practical tips for handling these challenges when they arise.

Understanding the significance of being prepared for RV breakdowns is the first step in mitigating their impact on your travels. RVs are complex machines with various components, systems, and moving parts, and breakdowns can occur for many reasons. Mechanical failures, electrical issues, tire blowouts, and plumbing problems are just a few examples of potential RV breakdowns that RVers may face. While breakdowns can be frustrating and inconvenient, knowing how to respond calmly and effectively can make all the difference in resolving the situation.

One of the key factors in dealing with RV breakdowns is staying informed and proactive about RV maintenance. Regular maintenance checks and inspections can help identify and address potential issues before they escalate into breakdowns. RVers should follow the manufacturer's recommended maintenance schedule for their specific RV model, which typically includes tasks such as engine and generator servicing, checking fluid levels, inspecting brakes, and assessing the condition of tires. Ignoring or delaying maintenance tasks can increase the risk of breakdowns and compromise safety.

Additionally, RVers should familiarize themselves with the operation of their RV systems and components. Knowing how to troubleshoot common problems and perform basic repairs can be invaluable on the road. RV manuals and online resources can provide guidance on the operation, maintenance, and troubleshooting of various RV systems, from electrical and plumbing to appliances and HVAC. Learning these skills can empower RVers to address minor issues promptly and avoid costly breakdowns.

Despite the best preventive efforts, breakdowns can still occur. Therefore, it's essential for RVers to carry the necessary tools and equipment for basic repairs and maintenance while on the road. A well-stocked toolkit should include items such as wrenches, pliers, screwdrivers, fuses, electrical tape, hose clamps, and a tire repair kit. These readily available tools enable RVers to address minor issues quickly and safely. It's also advisable to carry a fire extinguisher, a first-aid kit, and essential safety equipment as part of your emergency preparedness.

When an RV breakdown occurs, the first and most crucial step is to ensure the safety of yourself, your passengers, and other road users. Pulling over to a safe location, such as a rest area, a parking lot, or the shoulder of the road, is the immediate priority. Activate hazard lights, set up warning triangles or cones, and use reflective vests if necessary to alert other drivers to your presence. Ensuring the safety of everyone on board should be the primary concern before addressing the breakdown itself.

Once safety is ensured, RVers can begin diagnosing the issue. It's essential to remain calm and methodical in your approach. Start by identifying the symptoms of the breakdown and gathering information about what happened leading up to the issue. This information can be valuable when seeking assistance or discussing the problem with a mechanic or technician. RVers with knowledge of RV systems and components can use this information to conduct preliminary checks and troubleshooting to determine the cause of the breakdown.

In cases where the issue is beyond your ability to repair, seeking professional assistance is the next step. Having a reliable roadside assistance plan or RV insurance policy can be a lifesaver in such situations. Many RV insurance policies offer comprehensive coverage, including emergency roadside assistance, towing, and repair services. RVers should familiarize themselves with the terms and coverage limits of their insurance policies and keep the contact information for their insurer and roadside assistance provider readily available.

When contacting roadside assistance or a repair service, provide them with accurate information about your location and the nature of the breakdown. Be patient and communicate clearly; this will help expedite the response and ensure that the appropriate resources are dispatched to assist you. Remember that RV breakdowns can occur in remote or less populated areas, where assistance may take longer to arrive. Having food, water, and essential supplies on hand can be beneficial if you need to wait an extended period.

While waiting for assistance, RVers should take advantage of the time to assess their immediate needs and safety. If you have passengers or pets on board, ensure their comfort and well-being. Consider whether it's safe to remain in the RV or if it's better to wait outside. Use the time to review your insurance, warranty coverage, and any available roadside assistance benefits. Knowing what is covered and what you can expect from your service provider can help you make informed decisions during a breakdown.

In some cases, RVers may be able to continue their journey after a temporary fix or bypassing a non-essential component. However, exercising caution and prioritizing safety is essential when considering such options. Never attempt to make a repair or bypass a system if you are unsure of the consequences or if it compromises safety. It's always better to wait for professional assistance and proper repairs, even if it means a delay in your travel plans.

RVers should adopt proactive strategies that promote safe and trouble-free travel to minimize the risk of breakdowns. These strategies include conducting regular pre-trip inspections, maintaining recommended maintenance schedules, and staying informed about RV systems and components. RVers should also monitor their RV's performance while on the road, paying attention to any unusual noises, odors, or warning lights that may indicate a potential issue. Addressing minor problems promptly can prevent them from escalating into major breakdowns.

In conclusion, dealing with RV breakdowns is an inevitable part of RV travel, and being prepared for such situations is essential for a smooth and enjoyable journey. By prioritizing safety, staying informed about RV maintenance, carrying the necessary tools and equipment, and having access to reliable roadside assistance, RVers can navigate challenges on the road with confidence. While breakdowns can be stressful and disruptive, they can also be opportunities for learning and growth, as RVers gain valuable experience in handling unexpected situations. Ultimately, with the right mindset and preparedness, RVers can continue to embrace the spirit of adventure and discovery that makes RV travel so rewarding, even in the face of unexpected challenges.

Weather-related challenges

Recreational vehicle (RV) travel offers the freedom to explore the great outdoors while enjoying the comforts of home on wheels. While the appeal of RVing lies in the journey's spontaneity, RVers need to be prepared for the weather-related challenges they may encounter on the road. From extreme temperatures to severe storms, nature's elements can pose significant challenges during RV trips. In this section, we will explore the importance of weather preparedness for RVers, discuss common weather-related challenges, and provide practical tips for staying safe and comfortable while on the road.

Understanding the significance of weather preparedness is the first step in ensuring a successful and enjoyable RV trip. Weather can be unpredictable and can vary dramatically depending on your location and the time of year. Whether traveling through deserts, mountains, coastal regions, or forests, it's essential to be aware of the potential weather-related challenges and plan accordingly.

One of the most common weather-related challenges for RVers is extreme temperatures. High temperatures in summer can lead to uncomfortable conditions inside the RV, while frigid winter temperatures can pose a threat to both the RV and its occupants. RVers should equip their RVs with adequate heating and cooling systems to maintain a comfortable interior climate. This includes ensuring that furnaces, air conditioners, and ventilation systems work well. Additionally, having appropriate insulation and window coverings can help regulate interior temperatures and reduce the reliance on heating or cooling systems.

During hot weather, RVers should take steps to prevent overheating inside the RV. Park in shaded areas when possible, use reflective window covers, and avoid running appliances that generate excess heat during the hottest part of the day. Staying hydrated and wearing lightweight, breathable clothing is also essential to cope with high temperatures. In contrast, insulating the RV's water lines and tanks during cold weather can prevent freezing, and using skirting or thermal blankets around the RV's base can help retain heat.

Rain and storms are another weather-related challenge that RVers may encounter. Rain can lead to wet and muddy conditions, which can be particularly challenging for boondocking or staying in undeveloped areas. RVers should have proper rain gear, mud mats, and footwear to manage wet conditions outside the RV. Inside, leak-proof roof maintenance and window seals are critical to prevent water intrusion. Regularly inspect the RV's exterior for signs of wear and tear that could lead to leaks.

Severe weather events like thunderstorms, tornadoes, hurricanes, or blizzards can pose significant risks to RVers. It's essential to stay informed about weather forecasts and warnings for the areas you plan to visit and be prepared to alter your travel plans if necessary. Seek shelter in a sturdy building or designated storm shelter if severe weather is imminent. While RVs are equipped to withstand various weather conditions, it's safer to avoid traveling during extreme weather events whenever possible.

In winter, snow and ice accumulation can make RV travel treacherous. RVers should carry tire chains or snow cables and be proficient in their installation. Snow removal tools, such as shovels and ice scrapers, are also essential for clearing pathways and ensuring safe access to the RV. Insulating the RV's windows and doors can help retain heat and prevent drafts. Additionally, using specialized RV antifreeze in the plumbing system can protect against frozen pipes and water damage.

Fog is another weather-related challenge that can reduce visibility and make driving hazardous. RVers should exercise caution and reduce their speed when encountering foggy conditions. Using headlights, not high beams, and fog lights when equipped, can help improve visibility without causing glare. Staying a safe distance behind other vehicles and using reflective tape or markers on the RV can make it more visible to other drivers.

High winds can also present challenges during RV trips, particularly for larger RVs and trailers. Windy conditions can affect stability and control, making driving more challenging. RVers should be prepared to reduce their speed and pull over to a safe location if wind gusts become dangerous. Additionally, securing awnings, slide-outs, and any loose items outside the RV can prevent damage or accidents caused by strong winds.

Wildfires are an increasingly common weather-related concern for RVers, particularly in regions prone to drought and dry conditions. RVers should monitor wildfire alerts and evacuation notices and be prepared to leave the area if necessary. Keeping the RV's exterior and surroundings free of dry vegetation, leaves, and flammable materials can reduce the risk of ignition. It's also a good practice to have an emergency evacuation plan in place and to communicate with local authorities or campground staff for guidance during wildfire events.

In addition to the challenges posed by extreme weather conditions, RVers should also be prepared for changes in weather patterns that may affect their travel plans. Weather can be fickle, and unexpected shifts can lead to rain, snow, or temperature fluctuations. Having a flexible itinerary and alternative plans in case of adverse weather can help RVers adapt to changing conditions without disrupting their trip.

To effectively navigate weather-related challenges during RV trips, RVers should stay informed and utilize available resources. Monitoring weather forecasts through smartphone apps, weather websites, or a NOAA weather radio can provide timely information about upcoming weather conditions and warnings. Being aware of severe weather watches and warnings for your location is essential for taking appropriate action and staying safe.

Additionally, RVers can benefit from the wisdom and experiences of fellow travelers. Joining online RV forums and social media groups dedicated to RVing allows you to tap into the collective knowledge of the RV community. RVers often share their weather-related experiences, tips, and recommendations for dealing with specific weather challenges in various regions. Engaging with these communities can provide valuable insights and support when facing weather-related issues.

In conclusion, weather-related challenges are an inherent part of RV travel, and being prepared for them is essential for a safe and enjoyable journey. RVers should prioritize safety and comfort by equipping their RVs with appropriate heating and cooling systems, maintaining insulation, and carrying essential tools and equipment. Staying informed about weather forecasts and warnings, adapting travel plans when necessary, and having a flexible itinerary are strategies that can help RVers navigate changing weather conditions. By embracing weather preparedness as an integral part of their RV lifestyle, RVers can continue to enjoy the freedom of the open road while staying resilient in the face of nature's elements.

Health and safety on the road

Recreational vehicle (RV) travel embodies the spirit of adventure and exploration, allowing individuals and families to experience the freedom of the open road while enjoying the comforts of home. However, amid the excitement of RVing, it's crucial to prioritize health and safety on the road. Long hours of driving, exposure to varying weather conditions, and the potential for accidents or emergencies necessitate a proactive approach to safeguarding well-being during RV trips. This section will delve into the importance of health and safety while traveling in an RV, discuss common risks and challenges, and provide practical tips for ensuring a safe and enjoyable RV journey.

Understanding the significance of health and safety on the road is paramount for RVers. The RV lifestyle often involves extended periods of travel, which can result in physical and mental fatigue. Prolonged sitting while driving, irregular sleep patterns, and exposure to environmental factors can all impact health and well-being. Furthermore, the unfamiliarity of new locations, limited access to medical facilities, and the potential for accidents or injuries require a vigilant approach to health and safety.

One of the primary health concerns for RVers is the sedentary nature of long drives. Hours spent behind the wheel can lead to physical discomfort, muscle stiffness, and even the risk of blood clots. To mitigate these issues, RVers should practice regular stretching exercises and take breaks every few hours to walk around and maintain circulation. Ergonomic seating and lumbar support cushions can enhance comfort during extended drives. Additionally, maintaining proper posture and adjusting seat positions can reduce strain on the body.

Sleep quality and quantity are essential components of health and safety on the road. Irregular sleep patterns due to changing campsite locations or noisy environments can disrupt restful sleep. RVers should prioritize sleep hygiene by creating a comfortable sleeping environment within their RV. This includes using blackout curtains to block external light, employing earplugs or white noise machines to minimize disturbances, and maintaining a consistent sleep schedule as much as possible.

Furthermore, RVers should be mindful of their dietary choices and hydration while on the road. Travel often leads to changes in eating habits, with increased fast food or processed snacks consumption. Maintaining a balanced diet is essential by incorporating fresh fruits, vegetables, and whole grains into meals. Staying hydrated by drinking plenty of water is also crucial, especially in hot or dry climates. RVers should carry reusable water bottles and make an effort to monitor their fluid intake.

Another health consideration for RVers is the impact of changing weather conditions on well-being. Extreme temperatures, whether hot or cold, can affect comfort and safety. RVers should be prepared for temperature fluctuations by having appropriate clothing, blankets, and heating or cooling systems on board. In hot weather, avoiding heat-related illnesses is essential by staying hydrated, using sun protection, and seeking shade whenever possible. Preventing hypothermia and frostbite through proper insulation and clothing is paramount in cold weather.

Health and safety also extend to mental well-being during RV trips. The RV lifestyle can bring both excitement and stress, as travelers navigate new routes, encounter unexpected challenges, and adapt to changing environments. To maintain mental health, RVers should practice stress management techniques like mindfulness, deep breathing, and meditation. Staying connected with loved ones through regular communication can provide emotional support and reduce feelings of isolation.

Additionally, RVers should be aware of the potential for accidents or emergencies while on the road. RVs are complex vehicles that require safe driving practices and routine maintenance to prevent breakdowns or accidents.

RVers should adhere to speed limits, maintain a safe following distance, and avoid distractions while driving. Regular inspections of tires, brakes, and other critical components can identify issues before they become hazards.

RVers should have a well-equipped emergency kit in an accident or emergency. This kit should include first-aid supplies, flashlights, batteries, a fire extinguisher, essential tools, a tire repair kit, and emergency contact information. Familiarizing yourself with the location and operation of safety equipment, such as fire extinguishers and emergency exits, is essential. RVers should also know the location of nearby medical facilities and have a communication plan in case of emergencies.

Furthermore, RVers should have a comprehensive insurance policy that covers their RV and provides liability coverage. This insurance should include coverage for accidents, injuries, and property damage. Understanding the terms and conditions of the insurance policy is crucial for knowing what is covered and how to file a claim in case of an incident. RVers should always carry insurance documents, identification, and important medical information with them.

In addition to personal health and safety, RVers should also consider the safety of their RV and its systems. Regular maintenance checks and inspections are essential for ensuring that the RV operates safely and efficiently. RVers should follow the manufacturer's recommended maintenance schedule, which typically includes tasks such as engine and generator servicing, fluid checks, and brake inspections. Ignoring maintenance or neglecting necessary repairs can compromise safety and lead to breakdowns or accidents.

One critical aspect of RV safety is propane management. Propane is commonly used in RVs for cooking, heating, and powering appliances. RVers should have propane systems inspected regularly for leaks or malfunctions and should know how to shut off the propane supply in case of emergencies. Using propane-powered appliances safely, such as turning off the stove when not in use, can reduce the risk of accidents or fires.

Additionally, RVers should be cautious when operating slide-out rooms, leveling jacks, and awnings. These components require proper setup and use to prevent damage or accidents. Always follow the manufacturer's instructions and safety guidelines for these systems to ensure safe operation.

In conclusion, health and safety on the road during RV trips are paramount for a successful and enjoyable journey. RVers should prioritize physical and mental well-being by practicing healthy habits, managing stress, and staying connected with loved ones. Safety measures should include safe driving practices, routine RV maintenance, and being prepared for accidents or emergencies. By embracing a proactive approach to health and safety, RVers can confidently embark on their journeys, knowing that they are well-prepared to navigate the challenges and uncertainties of the open road while safeguarding their well-being.

CHAPTER X

Capturing Your RV Adventures

Photography tips

Photography is a powerful medium for capturing the essence and beauty of your RV trip. Whether you are a seasoned photographer or just someone who enjoys taking pictures on the go, some several tips and techniques can help you make the most of your photographic opportunities during your RV adventure.

First and foremost, it's essential to have the right equipment. While a high-end DSLR camera can deliver stunning results, you don't necessarily need expensive gear to take great photos. Many smartphones today come equipped with excellent cameras that can produce high-quality images. However, if you're passionate about photography, investing in a mirrorless or compact camera with manual settings can give you more creative control over your shots.

Once you have your equipment ready, it's time to focus on composition. One of the fundamental principles of photography is the rule of thirds. Imagine dividing your frame into nine equal parts with two horizontal and two vertical lines. The points where these lines intersect are prime locations to place your main subjects. This technique creates a balanced and visually appealing composition. When composing your RV trip photos, consider placing your RV or any interesting focal point along these lines to create more engaging and harmonious images.

Lighting is another critical aspect of photography. The best times to capture stunning photos during your RV trip are during the golden hours, which occur shortly after sunrise and just before sunset. During these times, the soft, warm light enhances your subjects and adds a beautiful touch to your photos. If you're photographing landscapes or your RV parked in a picturesque location, the golden hours can make all the difference in the world.

While the golden hours offer ideal lighting conditions, you can still take great photos during other parts of the day. When the sun is high in the sky, try to find interesting ways to work with the harsher light. You can experiment with shadows and highlights or use natural objects like trees to create shade and soft, dappled light. Additionally, using a polarizing filter can help reduce glare and make the sky and water appear more vibrant in your photos.

When it comes to photographing people during your RV trip, candid shots can capture genuine moments and emotions. Encourage your fellow travelers to be themselves and act naturally in front of the camera. By doing so, you can document authentic experiences and create lasting memories. However, don't shy away from posing your subjects when the situation calls for it. Directing your subjects can help you achieve a more polished and composed look in your portraits.

Another important consideration is the background. Pay attention to what's behind your subjects, as cluttered or distracting backgrounds can take away from the overall impact of your photos. Try to find clean, unobtrusive backgrounds that complement your subject and add to the story you want to tell through your images.

During your RV trip, you'll likely encounter various weather conditions. Embrace these conditions as opportunities to capture unique and dramatic shots. Rain can add a beautiful reflective quality to your images, while fog can create an enchanting and mysterious atmosphere. Don't be afraid to venture out and explore during different weather conditions, as they can lead to some of the most memorable and visually striking photographs.

It's also important to experiment with different perspectives and angles. Don't just take photos from eye level; get down low or climb up high to capture your subjects from unique vantage points. This can add depth and interest to your photos and help you see your RV trip from new and exciting angles.

Post-processing is an essential part of modern photography. Even if you're shooting with a smartphone, numerous apps can help you enhance your photos. Basic adjustments like cropping, exposure, and color correction can significantly affect the final result. However, remember that less is often more when it comes to editing. Overly processed photos can lose their authenticity, so strive for a balance that enhances your images without making them look unnatural.

Consider creating a photo journal or travel blog to document your RV trip effectively. This allows you to share your experiences with others and relive your journey through your photographs. Share your tips, stories, and insights to inspire fellow travelers and photography enthusiasts.

In conclusion, photography can be a fulfilling and creative way to capture the moments and memories of your RV trip. By having the right equipment, paying attention to composition, mastering lighting, and experimenting with different techniques, you can elevate your photography skills and create stunning images that truly reflect the essence of your adventure. Remember to embrace the beauty of different weather conditions, experiment with perspectives, and use post-processing to enhance your photos while maintaining their authenticity. So, grab your camera or smartphone, hit the road in your RV, and start capturing the extraordinary moments of your journey.

Journaling and documenting your travels

In an era dominated by digital technology and instant gratification, there's a certain allure to slowing down and embracing life's simple pleasures. RV (Recreational Vehicle) travel is one such pursuit that allows individuals to connect with nature, explore new destinations, and savor the journey at their own pace. While RV travel offers many benefits, one often-overlooked aspect is the practice of journaling and documenting your adventures along the way. Journaling during your RV travels is not just about putting pen to paper; it's a means of preserving memories, fostering self-reflection, and enhancing the overall travel experience.

With its freedom to roam wherever the road takes you, RV travel offers an unparalleled opportunity for exploration and discovery. Whether you're embarking on a cross-country road trip or simply escaping for a weekend getaway, each journey presents unique experiences and sights. Journaling allows you to capture these moments in vivid detail. As you document your travels, you create a lasting record of the places you've visited, the people you've met, and the feelings you've experienced. Your journal becomes a treasure trove of memories, allowing you to relive those adventures years later.

Beyond serving as a record of your travels, journaling also fosters self-reflection and personal growth. In the midst of the hustle and bustle of daily life, it's easy to become disconnected from oneself. RV travel, on the other hand, offers solitude and a chance to reconnect with your inner thoughts and feelings. Journaling becomes a therapeutic practice, providing a safe space to express your thoughts, fears, and dreams. It allows you to confront challenges and celebrate triumphs, leading to a deeper understanding of yourself and your journey.

Additionally, documenting your RV travels offers a platform for creative expression. You can infuse your journal with your unique artistic flair through words, sketches, photographs, or even scrapbooking. This creative journaling aspect adds an extra layer of enjoyment to your travels. As you write about the majestic landscapes you encounter, sketch the wildlife you observe, or compile a visual diary of your adventures, you'll find yourself engaged in the art of storytelling. Your journal becomes a canvas where you weave together the threads of your journey, creating a narrative that is uniquely yours.

In an age when digital photographs and social media updates dominate how we share our experiences, keeping a physical journal offers a more intimate and tangible connection to your travels. While Instagram posts and Facebook updates may garner likes and comments, the act of putting pen to paper creates a deeper and more personal connection with your experiences. It's a journey inward as much as it is a journey outward. The process of writing or sketching in your journal slows down time, allowing you to savor each moment and appreciate the beauty of the present.

Moreover, journaling and documenting your RV travels can be a valuable resource for future trips. Your journal becomes a travel guide filled with insights, recommendations, and tips that you can refer back to when planning new adventures or revisiting favorite destinations. It's a repository of lessons learned, hidden gems discovered, and mistakes to avoid. By recording the names of campgrounds, the best local eateries, and the most breathtaking hiking trails, you create a valuable resource not just for yourself, but for fellow travelers seeking inspiration.

You don't need to be a seasoned writer or artist to get started with journaling during your RV travels. All you need is a blank notebook and a willingness to embrace the process. You can begin by jotting down daily observations, describing the landscapes you pass through, or recounting memorable encounters with fellow travelers. Over time, you'll find your unique voice and style, and your journal will reflect your personal journey.

In conclusion, journaling and documenting your RV travels is a practice that enriches the travel experience in countless ways. It allows you to create a lasting record of your adventures, fosters self-reflection and personal growth, encourages creative expression, and provides a deeper, more intimate connection with your travels. In a world where the rush of modern life often overshadows the simple joys of exploration, journaling offers a way to slow down, savor the moment, and cherish the beauty of the open road. So, next time you embark on an RV adventure, pack your journal along with your camping gear, and let the pages of your diary become a testament to the wonders of the less traveled road.

Sharing your RV journey with others

Embarking on an RV (Recreational Vehicle) journey is not merely a means of exploring new destinations; it's a lifestyle that offers a unique blend of adventure, freedom, and self-discovery. While many individuals choose RV travel as a way to escape the hustle and bustle of daily life, it's also a journey worth sharing with others. Sharing your RV journey allows you to connect with like-minded travelers, inspire wanderlust, and create lasting memories with friends and family. Whether through social media, blogging, or face-to-face encounters, the act of sharing your adventures can enhance the overall RV experience in meaningful ways.

In an age when social media dominates our lives, bringing others along on your RV journey is easier than ever. Platforms like Instagram, Facebook, and YouTube offer a digital canvas to showcase your travels and connect with fellow adventurers. Posting captivating photos of scenic landscapes, cozy campfires, or delicious campsite meals can not only keep friends and family updated but also inspire them to embark on their own RV adventures. The visual storytelling aspect of social media allows you to convey the essence of your journey, evoking a sense of wanderlust in your audience.

Beyond social media, blogging has emerged as a popular medium for sharing detailed accounts of RV journeys. A well-crafted travel blog provides a platform to chronicle your experiences, share tips and recommendations, and connect with a global community of travelers. Through written narratives, you can offer insights into the places you've visited, the challenges you've overcome, and the lessons you've learned along the way. Your blog becomes a resource for both novice and seasoned RV enthusiasts, fostering a sense of camaraderie within the RV community.

One of the most profound benefits of sharing your RV journey is the opportunity to connect with like-minded individuals. RV travel attracts diverse people, each with their own stories and experiences to share. By documenting your adventures and engaging with others through social media or blogs, you open the door to meaningful connections and friendships. These connections can lead to memorable meet-ups and collaborations, enhancing the richness of your journey. It's not uncommon for RV enthusiasts to form close-knit communities, organizing rallies and gatherings to celebrate their shared passion.

Sharing your RV journey also provides a sense of accountability and motivation. When you have an audience eagerly following your adventures, it encourages you to explore new destinations, try new activities, and step out of your comfort zone. The act of sharing can serve as a catalyst for personal growth, pushing you to make the most of your RV lifestyle. It inspires you to seek out hidden gems, engage with local cultures, and embrace the spontaneity of the road.

In addition to connecting with fellow travelers, sharing your RV journey with friends and family can be a profoundly rewarding experience. RV travel offers a unique opportunity to create lasting memories with loved ones. Whether it's a family road trip, a reunion with friends, or a romantic getaway with a partner, the RV becomes a cozy home on wheels where bonds are strengthened and shared experiences become cherished stories. Sharing your journey with loved ones allows you to disconnect from the distractions of everyday life and connect on a deeper level.

Moreover, documenting your travels for future generations can be a powerful legacy. Your RV journey becomes a living history, a testament to the adventures you've undertaken and the places you've explored. Through photographs, stories, and mementos, you leave behind a treasure trove of memories for your children and grandchildren to discover and cherish. Your RV journey becomes a source of inspiration for future generations, encouraging them to explore the world with curiosity and wanderlust.

In conclusion, sharing your RV journey with others is a practice that enriches the RV experience in countless ways. It allows you to connect with like-minded travelers, inspire wanderlust, create lasting memories with friends and family, and leave behind a legacy for future generations. Whether through social media, blogging, or face-to-face encounters, sharing your adventures enhances the sense of community and camaraderie that defines the RV lifestyle. So, as you hit the open road in your RV, don't forget to share the beauty, the challenges, and the joy of your journey with others, for in doing so, you not only enrich your own experience but also inspire the wanderer in all of us.

CONCLUSION

As we reach the final chapter of "Voyages in Vans: A Traveler's Guide to RV Life in National Parks," I hope you've embarked on a journey of inspiration and discovery. This book was crafted to ignite your passion for RV travel, providing the tools and insights needed to embark on unforgettable adventures in national parks.

Throughout these pages, we've explored the world of RV life, from choosing the perfect vehicle for your needs to navigating the intricacies of national park exploration. We've delved into the art of setting up camp, cooking delicious meals in your mobile kitchen, and capturing the beauty of nature through your lens. We've celebrated the joy of connecting with fellow RVers and the thrill of encountering wildlife in their natural habitats. We've also discussed the challenges that may arise on the road and offered solutions to ensure your journey remains safe and enjoyable.

But beyond the practical advice and tips, "Voyages in Vans" has aimed to evoke a sense of wonder and appreciation for the world's national parks. These protected treasures are not just places to visit but sanctuaries of natural beauty, biodiversity, and cultural significance. They are windows into the Earth's history and a testament to the importance of preserving our planet's most precious places.

As you reflect on the knowledge and inspiration gained from this book, I encourage you to take the next step: embark on your own RV journey to explore the national parks that beckon to you. Dive into the adventure, savor the freedom of the open road, and immerse yourself in the beauty of our planet's most stunning landscapes. Whether you're seeking solitude in the wilderness, embarking on epic hikes, or simply relaxing by the campfire, may each moment be a reminder of our remarkable world.

Remember that "Voyages in Vans" is not just a book; it's a call to action. It's an invitation to embrace the wanderlust within you and to create your own stories, memories, and connections with nature. It's a tribute to the RV community and the countless travelers who have found solace, joy, and meaning on the road.

So, fasten your seatbelt, open your heart to the beauty of national parks, and let the road carry you to new horizons. The world is vast, and your adventure awaits. "Voyages in Vans" wishes you safe travels, incredible experiences, and a lifelong love affair with the wonders of RV life in national parks.

Thank you for buying and reading/ listening to our book. If you found this book useful/ helpful please take a few minutes and leave a review on the platform where you purchased our book. Your feedback matters greatly to us.